HEALTHY
Instant Pot Mini®
·COOKBOOK·

100 RECIPES FOR **ONE** OR **TWO** WITH
YOUR **3-QUART** INSTANT POT!

HEALTHY
Instant Pot Mini®
·COOKBOOK·

100 RECIPES FOR **ONE** OR **TWO** WITH YOUR **3-QUART** INSTANT POT!

Nili Barrett

ALPHA

Publisher Mike Sanders
Editor Alexandra Andrzejewski
Book Designer & Art Director Rebecca Batchelor
Photographer Daniel Showalter
Food Stylist Lovoni Walker
Recipe Tester & Nutritionist Julie Harrington, RD
Proofreaders Georgette Beatty and Monica Stone
Indexer Brad Herriman

First American Edition, 2020
Published in the United States by DK Publishing
6081 E. 82nd Street, Indianapolis, Indiana 46250

Text copyright © 2020 Nili Barrett
DK, a Division of Penguin Random House LLC
20 21 22 23 24 10 9 8 7 6 5 4 3 2
002-317285-AUG2020

Library of Congress Catalog Number: 2019950698
ISBN 978-1-4654-9269-2

Note: This publication contains the opinions and ideas of its
author(s). It is intended to provide helpful and informative material
on the subject matter covered. It is sold with the understanding
that the author(s) and publisher are not engaged in rendering
professional services in the book. If the reader requires personal
assistance or advice, a competent professional should be
consulted. The author(s) and publisher specifically disclaim any
responsibility for any liability, loss, or risk, personal or otherwise,
which is incurred as a consequence, directly or indirectly, of the use
and application of any of the contents of this book.

Trademarks: All terms mentioned in this book that are known to
be or are suspected of being trademarks or service marks have
been appropriately capitalized. Alpha Books, DK, and Penguin
Random House LLC cannot attest to the accuracy
of this information. Use of a term in this book should not be
regarded as affecting the validity of any trademark
or service mark.

DK books are available at special discounts when purchased
in bulk for sales promotions, premiums, fund-raising, or
educational use. For details, contact: DK Publishing Special
Markets, 1450 Broadway, Suite 801, New York, NY 10018
SpecialSales@dk.com.

Printed and bound in Canada

Photo on page 160 copyright © 2020 Nadley Doerge
Images © Dorling Kindersley Limited
For further information see: www.dkimages.com

A WORLD OF IDEAS:
SEE ALL THERE IS TO KNOW

www.dk.com

Contents

Introduction 6
Introducing the Instant Pot Mini 8
Getting to Know Your Appliance 9
Programs 11
Equipment 12
Using Your Instant Pot Mini 14

Breakfast 16
Sticky Plantain and Bacon Steel-Cut Oatmeal 18
Honeyed Apple Oatmeal 20
Maple Buckwheat Hot Cereal with Hemp Hearts 21
Down-Home Cheesy Grits with a Kick 23
Coconut Currant Breakfast Quinoa 24
From-Scratch Vanilla Bean Yogurt 25
Orange Marmalade 26
Spiced Chai 27
Honey Lemon Mini–Mason Jar Muffins 28
Banana Chocolate Chip Mason Jar Muffins 30
Blueberry Greek Yogurt Mason Jar Coffee Cakes 31
Levi's Chia Applesauce Baby Bundtlet 33
For-Charity Buttermilk Pancake Bites 34
Poached Salmon and Eggs with Yogurt Sauce 35
Sweet Potato Breakfast Egg Cups 36
Spinach Prosciutto Egg Bites 38
Easy-Peel Hard-Boiled Eggs 39

Entrées, Soups, and Stews 40
Greek Chicken Gyro Bowls 43
Chicken Bone Broth 44
Layered Chicken Enchilada Casserole 45
Rotisserie-Style Chicken and Lemony Rice 46
Taco Meatloaf Cups 47
Asian Chicken Lettuce Wraps 48
Lime-Cilantro Pulled Pork 50
Asian Plum Short Ribs 51
Cranberry Chicken 53
Cinnamon Apple Pork Tenderloin 54
Bacon and Mushroom–Covered Pork Chops 55
Buffalo Chicken–Stuffed Sweet Potatoes 56
German Sausage and Sauerkraut Dinner 58
Tangy Beef and Broccoli 59
Orange Marmalade Chicken 60
Zuppa Toscana One-Pot Pasta 61
Garlic Butter Shrimp Scampi 63
One-Pot Red Beans and Rice 64
One-Pot Chicken Teriyaki and Rice 65
Vegetarian Curried Lentil Stew 66
Minnesota Wild Rice Soup with Bacon 67
Restaurant-Style Ramen Bowls 68

One-Pot Pad Thai 70
Thai Peanut Pork Curry 71
Massaman Chicken Curry 73
Beef Stew with Parsnips 74
Classic Beef Stroganoff 75
Creamy Corn Chowder 76
No-Dairy New England Clam Chowder 77
Autumn Pumpkin Chili 78
White Chicken Chili 80
Red Lentil Chicken Stew with Quinoa 81
Caribbean-Inspired Pork and Plantain Stew ... 83
Nourishing Chicken Noodle Soup 84
Egg Drop Soup 85
Green Chile Pork and Potato Stew 86
Cheesy Broccoli and Rice Soup 87
Jalapeño Popper Soup with Sausage 88
Harvest Apple Butternut Squash Soup 90
Hungarian Mushroom Soup 91

Sides and Veggies 92
Pot-in-Pot White Rice 94
Fluffy Brown Rice 95
Quick Cauliflower Rice 96
Quinoa in a Snap 97
Kimchi Fried Rice 99
Curried Cauliflower with Raisins and Almonds ... 100
Cranberry Apple Quinoa Pilaf 101
Lemony Cauliflower Tabbouleh 102
Cut-the-Carbs Spaghetti Squash 104
Tuscan Polenta 105
Lemon Dill Creamer Potatoes 107
Easy Potato Cauliflower Mash 108
No-Fuss Black Beans 109
Soy Ginger–Glazed Carrots 110
Artichokes with Garlic-Herb Butter 112
Maple-Glazed Brussels Sprouts 113
Parmesan Green Beans with Bacon 115
Sweet and Sour Danish Cabbage 116
Cornbread Bundtlet 117

Snacks and Appetizers 118
Pickled Jalapeño Deviled Eggs 120
Brown Rice Dolmas 122
Meat Lovers Crustless Mini Quiche Bites 123
Sweet Chili Chicken Meatballs 125
Steamed Pork and Ginger Dumplings 126
Mu Shu Vegetable Dumplings 127
Mexican Stuffed Mini Peppers 128
Mini–Mason Jar Corn Dog Muffins 130

Renae's Favorite Hummus 131
Bacon and Bleu Cheese–Stuffed Mushroom Caps . 133
Cheesy Taco Dip 134
Basil and Greek Olive White Bean Dip 135
Creamy Pesto Chicken Dip 136

Desserts 138
Drunken Apples with Whiskey and Raisins 140
Honey-Vanilla Peach Topping 142
Chocolate Fondue Dip 143
Sticky Coconut Rice with Mango 145
Christmas Eve Cinnamon Rice Pudding 146
Lemon Olive Oil Polenta Cake 147
Simply Indulgent Mini–Mason Jar Cupcakes ... 148
Talia's Fudge-A-Licious Brownies 150
Blank Slate Cheesecake Cups 151
Matcha Mini Cheesecake 153
Pineapple Upside-Down Mason Jar Cakes 154
Nutty Mason Jar Carrot Cakes 155
Mochaccino Lava Cake 156

Index 158
Acknowledgments and About the Author 160

Introduction

What I love about the Instant Pot is that it is a secret weapon in the kitchen for making healthy, from-scratch meals with real unprocessed food. Life can be hectic, and home cooking can often fall by the wayside in favor of going through a drive-through or relying on processed frozen food at the end of a long day. Especially when cooking for just one or two people, it can be hard to find the motivation to spend the time in the kitchen that it takes to put together healthy, nourishing meals. The Instant Pot Mini is a wonderful tool to coax busy people back into the kitchen and help them streamline the cooking process, saving time and energy. I have seen first hand the Instant Pot Mini bring "real food" cooking back into the realm of possibility for so many people, from busy working parents, to the disabled and the elderly.

I began cooking with an Instant Pot when they first came on the market, and I quickly realized that this appliance would transform my cooking like no other piece of kitchen equipment had up to that point! It not only cooked up scrumptious meals ultrafast (while tasting like I had slaved all day in the kitchen!), the cooking time was so hands off that I was able to fix it and forget it and ended up enjoying lots of extra time. While dinner cooked, I could catch up on chores, play with my kids, or even run errands. Beans, which I used to have to remember to soak overnight, cook from dry to perfection within about 30 minutes in the Instant Pot; tough cuts of meat, which I used to have to tend to for the better part of the day, cook down to fall-apart tender within an hour or two. I am so grateful to have discovered the Instant Pot and am continuing to enjoy all of the benefits that it offers in my kitchen.

This book contains 100 recipes filled with nourishing, whole foods that are all perfectly scaled for the Instant Pot Mini. While developing these recipes, I took care to consider those who are on dietary programs (keto and vegan) and made sure to offer different substitutions to make these recipes work for you and your specific needs. So whether you're new to Instant Pot cooking or an old pro, my hope is that in this book you will find inspiration and motivation to get back into the kitchen, to cook with real foods from scratch, and to experience the joy and vibrancy that comes along with it.

–Nili Barrett

Introducing the Instant Pot Mini

The Instant Pot Mini provides all of the features of the original Instant Pot, but it's shrunken down into a sleek and compact 3-quart size. It's considered a multicooker, which means it replaces many different kitchen appliances, including a slow cooker, rice maker, yogurt maker, and, of course, a stovetop pressure cooker.

Perfect for One or Two

The 3-quart Instant Pot is a great option for those cooking for just one or two people, as well as anyone with limited counter space or kitchen storage. Three quarts is the perfect size to make just two servings so you're not left with more leftovers than you can manage! Most of the recipes in this book yield two servings, and in most instances they're easy to double in a 6-quart pot, if preferred (see page 15).

The versatility of the Mini allows full meals to be cooked all in one pot for easy clean up. It's also a great way to cook side dishes or desserts while keeping the stovetop and oven free for other courses of the meal. In this book, you'll find 19 fast and easy side dishes (starting on page 94) and 13 delicious desserts (starting on page 140) to complement your normal cooking routine.

Healthier Food, More Quickly

With this powerful little workhorse in the kitchen, you'll find it easier than ever to skip the drive-through on busy evenings. You can throw together healthy and delicious, from-scratch meals right at home using nutritious whole foods. The recipes you find in this book are brimming with natural, nutrient-dense ingredients, such as bone broth, beans, vegetables, meats, and fruits, as well as substitution options for those on specific dietary plans like keto or vegan. Whether you're looking to stay gluten or dairy-free, watch your carb intake, or eat a plant-based diet, you'll find lots of tasty options that will keep you on track with *your* healthy diet.

Under ordinary circumstances, the longer foods are cooked and the more water you put in a pot, the more nutrients are lost. However, by using a great amount of pressure with the Instant Pot, foods cook much more quickly, and the nutrients aren't leached out into boiling water. With pressure cooking, more nutrients remain intact in your food and the result is a healthier and more nourishing final dish—while still being perfectly cooked and tender!

Cooking Under Pressure

Using pressure to enhance cooking is a technique that has been around for hundreds of years. In the airtight container, moisture and steam are forced into the food rather than escaping the pot, giving you extremely tender and juicy results. Instant Pots are a far leap from traditional stovetop cookers; this modern appliance has 10 built-in and proven safety mechanisms to avoid mishaps and burns. Now with the Instant Pot, you can conveniently enjoy the time-saving and nutrient-retaining benefits of pressure cooking without the hassle of stovetop pressure cookers. Cooking foods under pressure not only helps them to cook up to 70 percent faster than with traditional methods (saving you lots of time in the kitchen!), but it also helps the food retain the moisture that is often lost in regular cooking.

Choosing Your Model

There are many Instant Pot models on the market from which to choose. I recommend choosing a model that includes a Yogurt button as well as handles that have a lid rest, such as the DUO series. Certain models feature a convenient pressure release button instead of a valve that has to be manually flipped between sealing and venting (see page 9). This button automatically sets the valve to the sealing position when the lid closes so you don't have to remember to flip it manually. For this feature, consider the DUO Nova series. To develop and test the recipes in this book, we used the DUO and the DUO Plus models.

Getting to Know Your Appliance

Understand how all of the parts of your Instant Pot Mini work together so that your pressure cooking is safe and effective. While cooking with the Instant Pot does have a learning curve, the time taken to master this little device will be well worth the effort.

Cooker Base   Features the control panel on the front and holds the inner pot. The base is not dishwasher safe. The outside should only be cleaned by gently wiping down with a wet towel or a gentle cleaner, and the inside should only be cleaned with a dry cloth.

Inner Pot   The stainless steel pot that fits into the base. Never attempt to use the Instant Pot without the inner pot in place. It is dishwasher safe.

Lid   Fits onto the base to create an airtight seal on the pot. In order to use any pressure cooking settings, the lid of the Instant Pot must be fully assembled and in place. On most models, the lid conveniently rests in the handles of the Instant Pot base to keep your counters clear. The lid is fully dishwasher safe.

Steam Release Valve   (Also called the *Pressure Release Valve*.) A weighty little valve that lets steam escape from the inner pot. It will be a bit wiggly when sitting in place, which is normal. On certain models, the steam release valve doubles as a handle, which acts as the *Quick Release Button;* it toggles back and forth to control whether the pot is in the "sealing" or "venting" position.

Steam Release Valve — Float Valve — Quick Release Button — Sealing Ring — Float Valve — Anti-Block Shield

OUTER LID   **INNER LID**

Sealing vs. Venting

The "sealing" position creates an airtight seal so the pot can come to pressure. The "venting" position allows air to flow freely through the lid. Anytime you are not pressure cooking (i.e., slow cooking) and don't need an airtight seal, you can set the valve to venting.

Quick Release Button   Controls whether the pot is in the "sealing" or "venting" position. Not all pots have a separate button for this (see *Steam Release Valve*). On many models, the quick release button automatically seals when you close the lid. To switch to venting, press the button down until it clicks.

Float Valve   The little metal pin on top of the Instant Pot lid. It pops up to indicate when the inner pot is pressurized, and it falls back down when the pressure has been released. When the pin is up and the pot is pressurized, the lid will be locked and unable to move until the pressure is released and the pin drops again. On the bottom of the lid, you'll see the bottom of the float valve, which is secured with a little silicone cap. You can remove the cap and take the float valve out of the lid for cleaning. Be sure that the float valve and the silicone cap are properly in place before cooking because the Instant Pot will not come to pressure without them.

Sealing Ring   A silicone ring that fits into the underside of the lid. The Instant Pot cannot come up to pressure without the sealing ring in place, so be sure that it's correctly installed before attempting to pressure cook. You can easily remove the sealing ring for cleaning. It sometimes retains the smells of very fragrant dishes cooked in the Instant Pot; to avoid inadvertently flavoring dishes with the sealing ring, you can purchase an extra one—one dedicated to sweet dishes, and the other for savory dishes.

Anti-Block Shield   A small metal cap on the underside of the lid that protects the underside of the steam release valve. The shield keeps the steam release valve from getting clogged with food during cooking. While it can stay in place most of the time, you should remove it for cleaning if the lid gets dirty.

Condensation Collector   A little plastic cup fitted into the back of the Instant Pot base. The condensation collector catches any liquid that makes its way around the top rim of the Instant Pot after cooking. Although the cup doesn't fill up often, it should be checked and cleaned regularly.

The Pressure Cooking Process

Once you understand all the parts of your Instant Pot, pressure cooking is a very simple process.

1. **Add your ingredients to the inner pot,** sautéing any meats or vegetables first, if desired.

2. **Make sure you have enough liquid in the pot,** about 1 cup, which enables pressure to build. The liquid content of your ingredients that will be released during cooking (i.e., the water content of mushrooms) counts toward this liquid minimum. Meats, fruits, and certain vegetables release a lot of liquid while cooking.

3. **Lock the lid and make sure the steam release valve (or quick release button) is set to the sealing position.** This makes sure the pot is airtight so it can build pressure. On some models, you seal the valve by turning the handle of the steam release valve. On other models, there is a quick release button that automatically seals the pot when you close the lid.

4. **Select your pressure cooking program, adjust to high or low pressure, and set the cook time.** Note that your altitude affects your cook time. The recipes in this book are designed for within 2,000 feet (610m) of sea level. If you are located more than 2,000 feet (610m) above sea level, increase the cook time by 5 percent for each 1,000 feet (300m) above sea level. For example, if you are at 3,000 feet (915m) above sea level, increase your cook time by 5 percent. For 4,000 feet (1,200m), increase by 10 percent, and so on.

5. **When the cook time is complete, release the pressure.** There are three ways to do this (see *Methods of Releasing Pressure*). Once the pressure is fully released and the pin drops down, you can remove the lid.

Methods of Releasing Pressure

After the pressure cook time is complete, the Instant Pot will still be pressurized, and the lid will remain locked until the pressure is released. (Never try to force the lid open while the pot is pressurized and the float valve is raised.) There are a few ways to release the steam and depressurize the pot; your recipe will tell you which method is appropriate for the best results.

The first method is Quick Release (QR). Immediately when the cook time is finished, turn the quick release button to the venting position or, depending on your model of Instant Pot, press the quick release button down until it clicks. Steam will pour out of the steam release valve very quickly until the pot is fully depressurized and the float valve drops down. Because food continues to cook while in a pressurized pot (even after the cook time is complete), a QR will prevent the food from overcooking. QR is great for items that are steamed with just a little bit of liquid in the pot, such as vegetables or boiled eggs.

The second method is Natural Pressure Release (NPR). With this method, after the cook time is complete, you allow the pot to sit and very slowly cool down until it fully depressurizes on its own. The amount of time it takes will depend on the ingredients in the pot. Full pots of soup and larger items may take 30 minutes to naturally release all the pressure, while smaller items with just a bit of liquid can take as short as 8 minutes. NPR is good for things that tend to foam, such as beans and grains, as well as meats that can lose too much moisture if the pressure is released too quickly.

The third method combines both NPR and QR. You allow the pot to cool down and release pressure naturally for a certain amount of time, then you quick release the rest of the pressure. This way you don't have to worry about foamy foods spraying from the valve if steam is released too quickly, but you also have the convenience of speeding up the rest of the release time so you're not waiting around.

Programs

The Instant Pot comes with many cooking programs designed for preparing a wide range of foods. Programs automatically begin a few seconds after you select them or after you press Start on certain models. The appliance conveniently stores cook times and pressure levels for programs you use often. You can cook most items with the manual Pressure Cook setting, but understanding the specifics of all of the different cooking programs can help you make the most of your Instant Pot. Note that the language of the buttons can change between models, and sometimes programs are added or dropped.

Pressure Programs

These programs use pressure to cook your food. The lid must be sealed for these to work. See your manual for information on preset cooking times.

Pressure Cook   The most common setting for cooking with the Instant Pot; it allows you manually to select the pressure level and cook time. Select High pressure for most meats, stews, or grains, or Low pressure for delicate foods such as vegetables.

Soup/Broth   Useful when you're making broth or soup with poultry because the pressure suppresses boiling motion, keeping your broth clearer. I always recommend High pressure.

Meat/Stew   Perfect for nonpoultry meats and stews. I always recommend High pressure.

Egg   Great for cooking eggs within the shells. I always recommend High pressure.

Rice   Best for medium- and long-grain white rice. This setting cooks at low pressure and the cook time is fully automated and not adjustable.

Bean/Grain/Chili   Makes cooking whole dried beans or grains quick and easy. Use High pressure for beans and chilis, and use Low pressure for quicker-cooking grains like quinoa.

Porridge/Oatmeal   Works well for cooking porridges like oatmeal or congee. I always recommend High pressure.

Steam   Great for any food that rests on a rack with water underneath. Use High pressure for foods such as eggs, and use Low pressure for delicate veggies.

Nonpressure Programs

These programs do not use pressure. The lid can be in the venting position (or you can use a glass lid). See your manual for information on preset cooking times.

Slow Cook   Use your Instant Pot instead of a slow cooker. Less/Low corresponds to a low slow cooker setting, Normal corresponds to a medium slow cooker setting, and More/High corresponds to a high slow cooker setting.

Sauté   Perfect for browning meats to lock in moisture and flavor before pressure cooking, simmering soups, or reducing liquid. Use Sauté to cook food just as you would use a pot on the stove. As a safety precaution, the maximum time for sauté is 30 minutes.

Yogurt   Use this setting for making homemade yogurt. Adjust to More for pasteurizing milk. While the milk is heating, "boiL" will appear on the display. When the milk has reached the correct temperature, the display will read "Yogt." After allowing the milk to cool to the correct temperature and adding the yogurt starter, adjust to Normal for fermenting the milk. The default fermentation time is set to 8 hours, but you can adjust the time as desired.

Keep Warm   This automatically turns on after pressure cooking is finished to keep your foods warm. The display timer will then begin counting up. Adjust to Less, Normal, or More to maintain foods at different temperatures for serving.

Equipment

Getting set up with the right accessories will make your Instant Pot cooking easy and successful. The inner pot is 7.8 inches (19.8cm) wide and 5 inches (12.7cm) tall; any oven-safe kitchenware that fits into the inner pot will work for pressure cooking. The following items are my favorites, and the ones I used to create the recipes in this book.

Silicone egg bite mold (with four wells)   These trays are perfect for cooking a variety of foods, such as egg bites, mini muffins, or poached eggs. When purchasing online, search for *3-quart Instant Pot egg bite molds.* My favorite product also comes with an egg steamer trivet with tall legs.

Steamer basket with feet   This comes in handy for anything that is cooked with steam and just a bit of water underneath the food. The feet keep the basket off the bottom of the pot and allow the water to sit underneath so steam can circulate. When purchasing online, search for *3-quart Instant Pot steamer basket.*

1-quart oven-safe bowl or baking dish   Oven-safe cookware, such as Pyrex or ceramic dishes, are great for pressure cooking. Certain recipes cook up best using the pot-in-pot cooking method—the baking dish sits on a trivet or steam rack, and water underneath provides the steam for cooking.

Stackable pans   These pans, specifically sized for the 3-quart pot, come in handy for cooking two foods at once. Used as a set, they work well for cooking dishes with similar cook times. My favorite method is to use just one of the pans in conjunction with the egg steamer trivet with tall legs—you can cook a recipe in the bottom of the inner pot, add the trivet, and place one of the stackable pans with another recipe on top. (For example, chicken curry in the bottom of the pot, and rice in the pan on top). When purchasing online, search for *3-quart Instant Pot stackable pans.*

Egg steamer trivet with tall legs   This may take a little work to find, but it will be well worth it! A tall-legged trivet allows you to cook a dish on the bottom of the Instant Pot at the same time as cooking another item perched above. When purchasing online, search for *3-quart Instant Pot egg steamer trivet with tall legs,* and look for one with 1½- to 2-inch (3.75–5cm) tall legs. My silicone egg bite molds came with a perfect trivet for this.

4- and 5-inch (10 and 12.5cm) push-bottom cake pans Use these pans for small-sized baked goods such as cheesecake, brownies, and lasagna.

Using aluminum foil for pan slings Foil is helpful when using the pot-in-pot cooking method so you can create makeshift handles to remove hot dishes from the pot. Fold a 15-inch (38cm) piece of foil lengthwise into fourths so that you have a skinny 15-inch (38cm) long strip. Lay the strip flat on the counter and place the pan on top of it in the center. Lift the two ends of the sling and use them as handles to transfer your pan in and out the Instant Pot. Fold the ends of the foil down toward the center of the pan so they're out of the way.

3-cup Bundt pan This miniature Bundt pan fits perfectly into the 3-quart Instant Pot and produces the most adorable little Bundtlet cakes!

Steam rack This handy accessory comes with all Instant Pot models. Use it to elevate cookware off the bottom of the pot so steam can circulate. This is great when you're cooking just one item, but I often prefer to use a trivet with taller legs so I can cook a second item beneath my pan or dish.

Tongs After cooking, anything in the inner pot is very hot. Use tongs to carefully remove food.

Silicone mitts or potholders After or during cooking, the rim of the inner pot can get very hot. To secure the inner pot while stirring or to remove the inner pot from the base after cooking, always use a pair of silicone mitts or a potholder.

8fl oz (235ml) wide-mouth canning jars It can be hard to find ramekins that can fit in the inner pot more than one at a time, but these wide-mouth canning jars fit two perfectly. I find that Kerr makes a perfect, easy-to-find variety.

4fl oz (120ml) canning jelly jars These 4fl oz jelly jars fit perfectly four at a time in the inner pot. They're great for making little single-serving desserts and breakfast treats.

Using Your Instant Pot Mini

Cooking in an Instant Pot bears much resemblance to traditional cooking methods, but there are a few key techniques to keep in mind.

Grains

With the Instant Pot, you can quickly cook side dishes such as rice or grains. I like to place the grains in a smaller pan above the main dish that is cooking in the inner pot. Place a tall trivet over the main dish, and place an additional pan with the grains on the trivet, allowing the full meal to cook at the same time.

Since grains can foam and be very thick, they have a tendency to stick or scorch when cooked directly in the inner pot, which causes a Burn error message. Cooking the grains in an elevated pan (whether you have a second main recipe cooking in the pot or not) allows the pot to build up enough steam to come up to pressure and avoids the possibility of the grains burning on the bottom of the pot.

To avoid a possible injury or making a mess, never fill the pot more than the halfway mark when cooking directly in the pot. Never use the quick pressure release method when cooking grains.

Meats

The Instant Pot is able to very efficiently break down proteins to tenderize meat while also locking in moisture. The end result is a fall-apart tender and juicy texture. To enhance flavor or lock in more moisture, it's a good idea to sear or sauté meats before pressure cooking. The Instant Pot makes it easy to do this all in one pot using Sauté mode.

Avoid the quick pressure release method when cooking cuts of meat because it can cause the meat to quickly release moisture and dry out; instead, allow pressure to release naturally for at least 5 minutes before quick releasing the rest of the pressure. Cook time for meat is dependent on the size or thickness of the piece(s) of meat you're cooking rather than the total weight in the pot. The thicker the pieces of meat, the longer they will take to cook. Always cut meat to the size specified in the recipes in order to ensure correct cook time.

Baked Goods

Some people are surprised to learn that you can make baked goods in the Instant Pot. Because it uses steam to cook, it's an ideal way to keep certain baked goods moist. Cheesecake, for example, comes out perfectly creamy all the way through without any dried-out edges.

When measuring ingredients for baked goods, especially flours, be sure to measure precisely. Ideally, use a food scale for the most accuracy. If you don't have a food scale available, spoon flour gently into the measuring cup so as not to compact it and overmeasure. Too much flour will result in a hard and dense finished product.

In this book, many baked goods use cassava flour as a healthier swap for wheat flour. Cassava flour is a grain-free, nut-free, gluten-free, and allergy-friendly flour that is easily found online and in many health food stores. Cassava flour is interchangeable in most recipes one-to-one with all-purpose flour.

Vegetables

Most vegetables cook very quickly under pressure, but there are a few tricks to avoid mushy veggies. When making dishes with a longer cook time, such as roasts and stews, consider adding in delicate vegetables at the end, turning the pot on **Sauté** mode to cook the vegetables just until the desired tenderness. When cooking vegetables on their own using a steaming basket or trivet, add 1 cup water underneath and use the **Pressure Cook** setting. For very delicate vegetables, you can choose Low pressure and set the cook time for as short as 0 minutes; this will cook the vegetables for just as long as it takes for the pot comes up to pressure before it switches to Keep Warm. This is often plenty of time to produce deliciously tender-crisp vegetables. In this case, a quick pressure release is a great choice to stop the cooking quickly before the food turns to mush.

The Timing

Timing for pressure cooking is important to understand so you can better plan your meals. For your convenience in choosing a recipe, this book lists the prep time, cook time, and total time required to make the dish from start to finish.

1. **Building pressure.** Once you select your cooking program and set a cook time, the Instant Pot starts heating up and building pressure. The cook time you selected will not actually start until the pot is hot and it has fully come up to pressure. The amount of time it takes for the pot to come up to pressure depends on the contents of the pot. Full pots of soup can take 20 minutes or more, while steaming items with only a little bit of water might only take 5 minutes.

2. **Cook time.** After the Instant Pot has fully come up to pressure, the cook time that you selected will begin to count down on the display screen.

3. **Releasing pressure.** When the cook time is finished, the pot will still be pressurized and the lid will be locked. The amount of time it takes to release pressure depends on the contents of the pot, usually anywhere from 10 minutes to 30 minutes. See page 10 for more information on releasing pressure.

Trouble Shooting

BURN STATUS MESSAGE   The Instant Pot has a safety feature that turns off the heat and presents a "Burn" error message if it senses that food is scorching on the bottom of the inner pot. This can happen for a variety of reasons, including cooking very thick items like tomato products or rolled oats. Sugars tend to scorch easily on the bottom of the inner pot, causing the error. Recipes in the book offer ways to avoid this, such as scraping up browned bits stuck to the bottom from sautéing before you start pressure cooking, and not stirring in tomatoes and sugars. The Burn message might also appear if there is not enough liquid in the pot or if the liquid has evaporated too quickly. This could be due to not enough liquid added in the pot initially or the liquid being cooked off quickly due to the pot not sealing and steam escaping for too long. Check that the silicone ring and the silicone cap on the inside of the lid are correctly installed.

FLOAT VALVE NOT COMING UP (POT ISN'T COMING TO PRESSURE)   If there isn't enough liquid in the pot, if the liquid is too thick, or if certain parts of the lid are not assembled correctly, the Instant Pot can have a hard time building pressure. If the cook time starts counting down on the display, but the float valve has not popped up to indicate that the pot is up to pressure, turn the Instant Pot off by pressing **Cancel.** Remove the lid and check that all of the pieces, especially the silicone ring, are properly installed. Add additional water to the pot, stir to release anything that might be stuck to the bottom of the inner pot, and try cooking again.

Doubling Recipes for a 6-quart Instant Pot

Most of the recipes in this book can be made in a 6-quart Instant Pot exactly as written, or with the ingredients doubled, if desired. When making a recipe in a 6-quart pot, ensure that there is at least 1½ cups liquid in the recipe. (Remember that all the liquid in the recipe counts toward this minimum, including the liquid that is released by meats and vegetables.) If the recipe does not contain at least 1½ cups, either double the entire recipe or add additional water until you reach the minimum. Cook times will remain the same.

All of the baked goods in this book can be made as written and cooked in a 6-quart Instant Pot. However, doubling these recipes is not recommended because increasing the size of the pans used will increase the necessary cook times.

Breakfast

Sticky Plantain and Bacon Steel-Cut Oatmeal

PROGRAM
Sauté (Normal), Pressure Cook (High)

RELEASE
Natural and Quick

Gluten-Free, Dairy-Free, Vegan Variation

If you're new to cooking plantains, start with this great recipe. They're a nutritious addition to any whole food diet. With a sticky brown sugar glaze and crunchy bacon crumbles, you'll surely fall in love with this ultrafilling breakfast!

Serves **2**   Serving Size **1 cup oatmeal and ½ cup topping**   Prep Time **15 mins**   Pressure Time **10 mins**   Total Time **45 mins**

½ cup steel-cut oats (certified gluten-free, if needed)

1½ cups water

¼ tsp salt

Full-fat coconut milk (optional), for serving

For the topping:

2 slices uncooked bacon, chopped

1 small, ripe yellow plantain, finely chopped

3 tbsp dark brown sugar

½ tsp ground cinnamon

⅛ tsp ground nutmeg

1 tsp arrowroot starch, or cornstarch

⅓ cup water

1. Prepare the topping. Select **Sauté (Normal).** When hot, add the bacon. Sauté until the bacon is browned and crispy. With a slotted spoon, remove the bacon to a paper towel–lined plate, leaving behind the rendered bacon fat. Set the bacon aside.

2. Add the chopped plantain to the inner pot and sauté for 3 to 4 minutes until beginning to brown. Add the brown sugar, cinnamon, and nutmeg, and stir to combine.

3. In a small bowl, stir together the starch and ⅓ cup water. Add the mixture to the inner pot and stir. Allow to simmer until slightly thickened and sticky, about 1 minute. Press **Cancel** to turn off Sauté. Transfer the plantain mixture to a small bowl and set aside.

4. In the inner pot, stir together the oats, 1½ cups water, and salt. Lock the lid and set the steam release valve to the sealing position. Select **Pressure Cook (High),** and set the cook time for **10 minutes.**

5. Once the cook time is complete, allow the pressure to release naturally for 10 minutes, then quick release any remaining pressure. Portion the oatmeal into two serving bowls. Top with equal amounts of the plantain mixture. Sprinkle with the bacon crumbles. Drizzle with coconut milk, if desired, and serve immediately.

TIP | Make it vegan: Omit the bacon and use 2 teaspoons coconut oil for sautéing the plantains.

NUTRITION PER SERVING (EXCLUDING COCONUT MILK):
Calories **409** • Total Fat **12.3g** • Total Carb **71g** • Fiber **5g** • Total Sugars **38g** • Protein **8g**

Honeyed Apple Oatmeal

This hearty breakfast dish comes by all of its sweetness naturally and is perfect for a crisp fall morning. All-natural honey and your favorite variety of apple combine to make a delicious topper for this satisfying pot of goodness.

PROGRAM
Sauté (More),
Pressure Cook (High)

RELEASE
Natural and Quick

Gluten-Free

Serves **2**   Serving Size **1½ cups oatmeal and ⅓ cup topping**   Prep Time **10 mins**   Pressure Time **8 mins**   Total Time **35 mins**

1 cup old-fashioned rolled oats (certified gluten-free, if needed)

2–2½ cups water

¼ tsp salt

Milk or cream (optional), for serving

For the apple topping:

2 tsp salted butter

1 apple, cored and finely chopped

2 tbsp honey

½ tsp pure vanilla extract

Pinch of salt

1. Prepare the apple topping. Select **Sauté (More).** When hot, add the butter. Once the butter is melted and bubbling, add the apples and sauté for 3 to 4 minutes until they begin to soften.

2. Add the honey, vanilla, and pinch of salt, and sauté for 1 minute more. Press **Cancel** to turn off Sauté. Transfer the apple topping to a small bowl and set aside.

3. Place the steam rack in the inner pot and add 1 cup water. In a separate 1-quart (1l), oven-safe bowl or baking dish that fits in the inner pot, mix together the oats, 2 cups water (or 2½ cups for thinner oatmeal), and salt. Place the baking dish on the steam rack.

4. Lock the lid and set the steam release valve to the sealing position. Select **Pressure Cook (High),** and set the cook time for **8 minutes.**

5. Once the cook time is complete, allow the pressure to release naturally for 5 minutes, then quick release any remaining pressure. Portion the oatmeal into two serving bowls. Top with equal amounts of the apple topping, drizzle with milk or cream, if desired, and serve immediately.

TIP | If you like a little tartness, choose a green variety of apple, such as Granny Smith. If you enjoy sweeter varieties, opt for a Fuji or Gala. Try with pear instead of apple for a yummy variation.

Rolled oats have a tendency to scorch on the bottom of the inner pot. To avoid this, this recipe uses the "pot-in-pot" cooking method.

To make the dish easier to remove from the Instant Pot after cooking, make a sling for your bowl with foil (page 13).

NUTRITION PER SERVING (EXCLUDING MILK OR CREAM FOR SERVING):
Calories **302** • Total Fat **6.6g** • Total Carb **58g** • Fiber **6g** • Total Sugars **27g** • Protein **6g**

Maple Buckwheat Hot Cereal with Hemp Hearts

This creamy, maple-sweetened buckwheat cereal is a great way to get out of a breakfast rut. A sprinkle of hemp hearts at the end adds a delicious and nutty flavor and also provides a variety of nutrients and essential fats.

PROGRAM
Pressure Cook (High)

RELEASE
Natural and Quick

Gluten-Free, Dairy-Free, Vegan

Serves **2**   Serving Size **about 1 cup**   Prep Time **5 mins**   Pressure Time **8 mins**   Total Time **30 mins**

½ cup dry Bob's Red Mill Creamy Buckwheat Hot Cereal

1½–2 cups water

3 tbsp pure maple syrup, divided

½ tsp ground cinnamon

½ tsp pure vanilla extract

⅛ tsp salt

2 tbsp full-fat coconut milk

2 tsp hemp hearts (also called *hulled hemp seeds*)

1. Place the steam rack in the inner pot and add 1 cup water. In a separate 1-quart (1l), oven-safe bowl or baking dish that fits in the inner pot, mix together the buckwheat cereal, 1½ cups water (or 2 cups for thinner cereal), 1 tablespoon maple syrup, cinnamon, vanilla, and salt. Place the baking dish, uncovered, on the steam rack.

2. Lock the lid and set the steam release valve to the sealing position. Select **Pressure Cook (High),** and set the cook time for **8 minutes.**

3. Once the cook time is complete, allow the pressure to release naturally for 5 minutes, then quick release any remaining pressure.

4. Portion the cereal into two serving bowls. Drizzle each with 1 tablespoon maple syrup and 1 tablespoon coconut milk. Sprinkle each with 1 teaspoon hemp hearts. Serve immediately.

TIP | Thick porridges have a tendency to scorch on the bottom of the inner pot. To avoid scorching, this recipe uses the "pot-in-pot" cooking method.

If you can't find preground buckwheat hot cereal, make your own by pulsing raw buckwheat groats in a blender until they are the texture of coarsely ground cornmeal.

To make the dish easier to remove from the Instant Pot after cooking, make a sling for your bowl with foil (page 13).

NUTRITION PER SERVING:

Calories **269** • Total Fat **4.7g** • Total Carb **54g** • Fiber **1g** • Total Sugars **18g** • Protein **4g**

Down-Home Cheesy Grits with a Kick

PROGRAM
Pressure Cook (High)

RELEASE
Natural and Quick

Gluten-Free

Send your taste buds on a trip down South with this take on a traditional Southern breakfast. With velvety Cheddar cheese and a kick of spice, this gluten-free breakfast is sure to wake you up in the morning.

Serves **2**   Serving Size **1 cup grits and 1 poached egg**   Prep Time **5 mins**   Pressure Time **10 mins**   Total Time **25 mins**

1 medium jalapeño, deseeded and minced

½ cup dry coarsely ground corn grits (also called *polenta*, not quick grits)

2 cups water

1 tsp salt

⅛ tsp smoked paprika

¼ tsp black pepper

¼ tsp red pepper flakes

¼ cup shredded Cheddar cheese

2 tbsp cream cheese

2 poached eggs (page 35)

1. In the inner pot, stir together the jalapeño, grits, 2 cups water, salt, paprika, pepper, and red pepper flakes. Lock the lid and set the steam release valve to the sealing position. Select **Pressure Cook (High),** and set the cook time for **10 minutes.**

2. Once the cook time is complete, allow the pressure to release naturally for 5 minutes, then quick release any remaining pressure. Stir in the Cheddar and cream cheese until melted and smooth.

3. Portion into two serving bowls. Rinse out the inner pot and prepare the poached eggs (see instructions on page 35). Top each portion with a poached egg, and serve immediately.

TIP Want it extra spicy? Double the red pepper flakes.

Very coarsely ground grits work the best for this recipe. More finely ground cornmeal can become too thick and scorch on the bottom of the inner pot, causing a Burn error message. If your grits are a finer grind, add an additional ½ cup water.

NUTRITION PER SERVING:

Calories **334** • Total Fat **16.5g** • Total Carb **33g** • Fiber **3g** • Total Sugars **1g** • Protein **14g**

Coconut Currant Breakfast Quinoa

PROGRAM
**Sauté (More),
Pressure Cook (Low)**

RELEASE
Natural and Quick

Gluten-Free, Dairy-Free, Vegan Variation

Quinoa makes an unexpected yet delicious base to this warm coconut breakfast bowl. Coconut is a well-known superfood with many health benefits, and it appears in this hot cereal recipe in several forms.

Serves **2**   Serving Size **about 1¼ cups**   Prep Time **10 mins**   Pressure Time **2 mins**   Total Time **30 mins**

¼ cup unsweetened shredded coconut

1 tsp coconut oil

3 tbsp dried currants

2 tbsp honey

½ tsp ground cinnamon

⅛ tsp ground cardamom

Pinch of salt

1¾ cups water

¾ cup quinoa

6 tbsp full-fat coconut milk

1. Select **Sauté (More).** When hot, add the shredded coconut and dry toast for about 4 minutes, stirring often, until lightly browned. Remove the toasted coconut from the inner pot and set aside.

2. Add the coconut oil, currants, honey, cinnamon, cardamom, and salt to the inner pot, and toss until the coconut oil is melted and the currants are coated with the spices. Add 1¾ cups water and bring up to a simmer. Stir in the quinoa. Press **Cancel.**

3. Lock the lid and set the steam release valve to the sealing position. Select **Pressure Cook (Low),** and set the cook time for **2 minutes.**

4. Once the cook time is complete, allow the pressure to release naturally for 5 minutes, then quick release any remaining pressure.

5. Portion the quinoa into two serving bowls. Drizzle each with 3 tablespoons coconut milk and sprinkle with the toasted coconut. Serve immediately.

TIP | Check your package of quinoa to see if it is prewashed. If not, rinse well with a fine-mesh strainer before cooking. This removes the bitter, naturally occurring saponins.

Make it vegan: Substitute your favorite vegan sweetener for the honey.

NUTRITION PER SERVING:
Calories **631** • Total Fat **33.5g** • Total Carb **77g** • Fiber **10g** • Total Sugars **28g** • Protein **12g**

From-Scratch Vanilla Bean Yogurt

Teeming with live cultures, homemade yogurt is a delicious way to get beneficial probiotics into your diet. Enjoy this hand-crafted, vanilla-scented yogurt with some raw honey, fresh berries, and granola for a delightful breakfast treat.

PROGRAM
Yogurt (More), Yogurt (Normal)

RELEASE
None

Gluten-Free

Makes **4 cups**   Serving Size **1 cup**   Prep Time **1 hour**   Cook Time **8 hours**   Total Time **14 hours**

1qt (1l; about 4 cups) whole milk (or low-fat milk, if desired)

2 tbsp favorite high-quality plain yogurt with live active cultures (to serve as the yogurt starter)

1 vanilla bean pod

1. Add the milk to the inner pot and lock the lid. You will not use pressure, so the steam release valve can be left in either the sealing or venting position. Select **Yogurt (More).** The display will read "boiL" and the Instant Pot will heat the milk to 185°F (85°C) to sterilize.

2. When the milk has reached the correct temperature, the display will read "YoGt." Press **Cancel** and open the lid. Remove the inner pot from the base and place on a wire rack. Cool the milk until it reaches 115°F (45°C), or is just slightly warm to the touch. (This can take 30 to 45 minutes.) If a skin forms on the surface, skim it off with a spoon.

3. While the milk is cooling, add the yogurt starter to a small bowl. Slice the vanilla bean pod in half lengthwise. With the edge of the knife, scrape out the vanilla seeds. Place the seeds in the bowl with the yogurt starter.

4. Once cooled to the correct temperature, remove ¼ cup warm milk and whisk it gently into the yogurt starter and vanilla seeds until smooth. Return the mixture to the inner pot and stir to combine.

5. Place the inner pot back into the Instant Pot base and lock the lid. Again, the steam release valve can be left in either the sealing or venting position. Select **Yogurt (Normal),** and set the incubation time to **8 hours.**

6. Once the incubation time is complete, remove the inner pot from the base, cover with a lid or plastic wrap, and transfer to the refrigerator. Chill undisturbed for at least 4 hours. Before serving, stir to disperse the vanilla seeds. Store in lidded jars in the refrigerator for up to 2 weeks.

TIP | Save 2 tablespoons yogurt from each batch you make so that you have starter ready for your next batch. You'll never have to purchase premade yogurt again!

For a tarter, thicker yogurt, increase the incubation time to 12 hours. For a sweeter, thinner yogurt, decrease the incubation time to 6 hours.

Easily double the recipe to make 8 servings at a time.

NUTRITION PER SERVING:
Calories **157** • Total Fat **8.3g** • Total Carb **12g** • Fiber **0g** • Total Sugars **12g** • Protein **9g**

Orange Marmalade

The perfect combination of sweet and bitter, this mouthwatering citrus spread is sure to bring sunshine to your breakfast table. It's simple to prepare and a great way to use up a surplus of oranges.

PROGRAM
**Pressure Cook (High),
Sauté (More)**

RELEASE
Natural and Quick

**Gluten-Free, Dairy-
Free, Vegan**

Makes **about
2 cups**   Serving Size **2 tbsp**   Prep Time **15 mins**   Pressure Time **10 mins**   Total Time **1 hour 30 mins**

1lb (450g) Valencia oranges
 (or other thin-skinned variety,
 about 3 small)
1¼ cup granulated sugar
1 cup water

1. Rinse and dry the oranges. Using a mandoline slicer or a sharp knife, slice the oranges into rounds as thinly as possible. Cut the rounds into sixths and transfer to the inner pot, along with any juice that is released. Add the sugar and 1 cup water.

2. Lock the lid and set the steam release valve to the sealing position. Select **Pressure Cook (High),** and set the cook time for **10 minutes.**

3. Once the cook time is complete, allow the pressure to release naturally for 5 minutes, then quick release any remaining pressure. Press **Cancel** to turn off Keep Warm.

4. Select **Sauté (More)** and bring to a simmer. Stirring occasionally, allow the marmalade to simmer for 25 minutes until the liquid becomes thick and syrupy. Stir more frequently in the final 10 minutes of cook time as the mixture thickens. Remove the inner pot from the Instant Pot and allow the marmalade to cool. Transfer to a lidded glass jar and store in the refrigerator. Serve when fully chilled. Store in the refrigerator for up to 1 month.

TIP | If you enjoy your marmalade on the bitter side, choose an orange with a thicker skin.

For a delicious twist, try substituting tangerines or blood oranges.

Marmalade makes a wonderful spread for toast or stir-in for homemade yogurt (page 25). It can even be used in savory dishes like Orange Marmalade Chicken (page 60).

NUTRITION PER SERVING:
Calories **74** • Total Fat **0g** • Total Carb **19g** • Fiber **1g** • Total Sugars **16g** • Protein **0g**

Spiced Chai

Pressure cooking extracts all of the essence of the chai spices before the tea leaves are added for steeping. This allows the full, spicy flavor to be enjoyed without oversteeping the tea leaves.

PROGRAM
Pressure Cook (High)

RELEASE
Quick

Gluten-Free, Dairy-Free, Vegan

Serves **2**   Serving Size **about 12fl oz (350ml)**   Prep Time **5 mins**   Pressure Time **5 mins**   Total Time **25 mins**

3 cups water

1 star anise pod

8 cardamom pods

¼ tsp whole black peppercorns

¼ tsp allspice berries

¼ tsp whole cloves

1 cinnamon stick

1in (2.5cm) piece fresh ginger, sliced

3 tsp bulk black tea leaves, or 2 black tea bags

2 tbsp honey, or to taste

¼ cup full-fat coconut milk (optional)

1. In the inner pot, combine 3 cups water, star anise, cardamom, peppercorns, allspice, cloves, cinnamon stick, and ginger. Lock the lid and set the steam release valve to the sealing position. Select **Pressure Cook (High),** and set the cook time for **5 minutes.**

2. Once the cook time is complete, quick release the pressure. Add the tea leaves and allow to steep for 5 minutes.

3. Add the honey and coconut milk, if using, and stir until the honey melts.

4. Using a fine-mesh strainer, strain out and discard the spices and tea leaves. Pour the tea into 2 large mugs and serve immediately.

TIP | This recipe works wonderfully with any plain black tea. For variety, try it with green, oolong, or Darjeeling.

Try doubling this chai recipe and storing the extra in the refrigerator. Enjoy over ice with milk or coconut milk for a delicious iced chai latte, or quickly reheat in the microwave for an afternoon pick-me-up.

NUTRITION PER SERVING (EXCLUDING COCONUT MILK):

Calories **75** • Total Fat **0.2g** • Total Carb **20g** • Fiber **1g** • Total Sugars **17g** • Protein **0g**

Honey Lemon
Mini–Mason Jar Muffins

PROGRAM
Pressure Cook (High)

RELEASE
Natural and Quick

Gluten-Free

The bright flavors in these sweet little morsels are sure to delight. Made with Greek yogurt, these muffins pack a protein punch and make a great breakfast or a perfect pick-me-up afternoon snack.

Makes **4 mini muffins**   Serving Size **2 mini muffins**   Prep Time **10 mins**   Pressure Time **12 mins**   Total Time **40 mins**

¼ cup plain full-fat Greek yogurt

½ tsp lemon extract

Zest of ¼ lemon

1 large egg

2 tbsp honey

⅓ cup (43g) cassava flour

¼ tsp baking soda

⅛ tsp salt

For the glaze:
4 tsp powdered sugar

½ tsp lemon juice

Zest of ¼ lemon

1. In a small bowl, whisk together the yogurt, lemon extract, lemon zest, egg yolk, and honey.

2. In a medium bowl, stir together the cassava flour, baking soda, and salt. Gently stir the yogurt mixture into the flour mixture until just combined.

3. Spray 4 (4fl oz; 120ml) canning jars with nonstick spray, and gently divide the batter equally between them.

4. Place the steam rack in the inner pot and add 1 cup water. Place the jars on the rack and rest the flat canning lid on top of each to keep out excess moisture. (There is no need to screw on the ring.)

5. Lock the lid and set the steam release valve to the sealing position. Select **Pressure Cook (High),** and set the cook time for **12 minutes.**

6. Meanwhile, make the glaze. In a small bowl, whisk together the powdered sugar, lemon juice, and lemon zest until smooth.

7. Once the cook time is complete, allow the pressure to release naturally for 5 minutes, then quick release any remaining pressure. Remove the lids and allow the muffins to cool in the jars on a wire rack for 5 minutes. Run a butter knife around the inside edges of the jars to make them easier to remove. Pop them out of the jars and allow to cool on the wire rack for 15 minutes more. Place on a serving tray, drizzle with glaze, and serve immediately.

TIP   For an almond poppy seed variation, substitute almond extract for the lemon extract, omit the lemon zest, and add ½ teaspoon poppy seeds to the batter. For the glaze, use 1 teaspoon milk in place of the lemon juice, and omit the lemon zest. Sprinkle the glazed muffins with sliced almonds, and enjoy.

For best results, use a food scale to accurately measure flours. If you do not have a food scale, gently spoon the flour into your measuring cup so as not to compact it. Inaccurately measuring flour can leave you with a hard and dense finished product.

NUTRITION PER SERVING:
Calories **209** • Total Fat **2.8g** • Total Carb **43g** • Fiber **2g** • Total Sugars **23g** • Protein **5g**

Banana Chocolate Chip Mason Jar Muffins

PROGRAM
Pressure Cook (High)

RELEASE
Quick

**Gluten-Free,
Dairy-Free**

The coconut oil gives these scrumptious muffins a generous serving of healthy fat and keeps them dairy-free. Indulge in the perfect flavor combination of bananas and chocolate, freshly baked, right from your Instant Pot.

Makes **2 muffins**   Serving Size **1 muffin**   Prep Time **10 mins**   Pressure Time **16 mins**   Total Time **46 mins**

1 tbsp coconut oil, melted

½ very ripe medium banana, mashed

1 tbsp coconut sugar

½ tsp pure vanilla extract

1 large egg yolk

¼ cup (32g) cassava flour

¼ tsp ground cinnamon

⅛ tsp salt

½ tsp baking soda

2 tbsp semisweet, dairy-free chocolate chips

1. In a small bowl, whisk together the coconut oil, mashed banana, coconut sugar, vanilla, and egg yolk.

2. In a separate small bowl, stir together the cassava flour, cinnamon, salt, and baking soda. Gently stir the flour mixture into the banana mixture until just combined.

3. Spray 2 (8fl oz; 235ml) wide-mouth canning jars with nonstick spray. Gently pour half of the batter into each. Top each with 1 tablespoon chocolate chips.

4. Place the steam rack in the inner pot and add 1 cup water. Place the jars on the steam rack and rest the flat canning lid on top of each to keep out excess moisture. (There is no need to screw on the ring.)

5. Lock the lid and set the steam release valve to the sealing position. Select **Pressure Cook (High),** and set the cook time for **16 minutes.**

6. Once the cook time is complete, quick release the pressure. Allow the muffins to cool uncovered in the jars on a wire rack for at least 10 minutes. Run a butter knife around the inside edges of the jars to make them easier to remove. Serve warm or fully cooled. Store in an airtight container at room temperature for up to 3 days.

TIP | Screw the lid on the jar after the muffins have cooled for a quick and easy breakfast on the go. Warm up the muffin in the microwave for a few seconds before serving.

For best results, use a food scale to accurately measure flours. If you do not have a food scale, gently spoon the flour into your measuring cup so as not to compact it. Inaccurately measuring flour can leave you with a hard and dense finished product.

NUTRITION PER SERVING:
Calories **276** • Total Fat **13.1g** • Total Carb **40g** • Fiber **4g** • Total Sugars **16g** • Protein **3g**

Blueberry Greek Yogurt Mason Jar Coffee Cakes

PROGRAM
Pressure Cook (High)

RELEASE
Natural and Quick

Gluten-Free

This decadent breakfast is enough to make any morning a special occasion. With wild blueberries and buttery melt-in-your-mouth streusel topping, you won't even notice that these Greek yogurt coffee cakes are grain-free!

Makes **2 mini coffee cakes** Serving Size **1 mini coffee cake** Prep Time **5 mins** Pressure Time **20 mins** Total Time **55 mins**

2 tbsp salted butter, softened

2 tbsp coconut sugar

1 large egg yolk

½ tsp pure vanilla extract

¼ cup plain full-fat Greek yogurt

¼ cup (32g) cassava flour

½ tsp baking soda

¼ tsp salt

2 tbsp frozen wild blueberries

For the streusel topping:

1 tbsp salted butter, melted

2 tbsp dark brown sugar

⅛ tsp salt

3 tbsp (24g) cassava flour

1. In a small bowl, cream together with a spoon the butter and coconut sugar. Add the egg yolk, vanilla, and yogurt, and mix until smooth.

2. In a separate small bowl, stir together the cassava flour, baking soda, and salt. Gently stir the flour mixture into the yogurt mixture. Fold in the blueberries. Spray 2 (8fl oz; 235ml) wide-mouth canning jars with nonstick spray. Gently pour half of the batter into each jar.

3. Prepare the streusel topping. In a small bowl, stir together the butter, brown sugar, salt, and cassava flour until crumbly. Top each coffee cake with half of the topping mixture.

4. Place the steam rack in the inner pot and add 1 cup water. Place the jars on the steam rack and rest the flat canning lid on top of each to keep out excess moisture. (There is no need to screw on the ring.) Lock the lid and set the steam release valve to the sealing position. Select **Pressure Cook (High),** and set the cook time for **20 minutes.**

5. Once the cook time is complete, allow the pressure to release naturally for 5 minutes, then quick release any remaining pressure. Remove the lids and allow the coffee cakes to cool in the jars on a wire rack for at least 10 minutes. Run a butter knife around the inside edges of the jars to make them easier to remove. Serve warm or completely cooled. Store at room temperature in an airtight container for up to 3 days.

TIP | Customize the flavors by adding different fruits or nuts in place of the blueberries. Try chopped peaches or pecans.

For best results, use a food scale to accurately measure flours. If you do not have a food scale, gently spoon the flour into your measuring cup so as not to compact it. Inaccurately measuring flour can leave you with a hard and dense finished product.

NUTRITION PER SERVING:
Calories **363** • Total Fat **19.5g** • Total Carb **46g** • Fiber **3g** • Total Sugars **20g** • Protein **4g**

Levi's Chia Applesauce Baby Bundtlet

PROGRAM
Pressure Cook (High)

RELEASE
Natural and Quick

**Gluten-Free,
Dairy-Free**

This fragrant cake is naturally sweetened with applesauce and coconut sugar and provides a serving of healthy fat from the coconut oil. The delicious, chewy texture of the Bundtlet comes from the chia seeds, also providing some extra fiber.

Serves **4**   Serving Size **¼ Bundtlet**   Prep Time **15 mins**   Pressure Time **30 mins**   Total Time **1 hour 15 mins**

2 tsp chia seeds

2 tbsp water

¾ cup (96g) cassava flour

1 tsp baking soda

½ tsp salt

¼ cup melted coconut oil, cooled slightly

½ cup unsweetened applesauce

½ cup coconut sugar

1 tsp pure vanilla extract

1 large egg

½ tsp avocado oil or olive oil

1. In a small bowl, stir together the chia seeds and 2 tablespoons water. Allow to gel while preparing the rest of the ingredients.

2. In a medium bowl, combine the cassava flour, baking soda, and salt. In another small bowl, whisk together the coconut oil, applesauce, coconut sugar, vanilla, and egg. Add the gelled chia seeds, and whisk to combine.

3. Add the applesauce mixture to the flour mixture. Gently stir until just combined.

4. Using your fingers, grease a 3-cup Bundt pan with the avocado or olive oil, distributing it evenly to cover all of the surfaces inside the pan. Pour in the batter and spread evenly. Place the steam rack in the inner pot and add 1 cup water. Place the pan on the steam rack.

5. Lock the lid and set the steam release valve to the sealing position. Select **Pressure Cook (High),** and set the cook time for **30 minutes.**

6. Once the cook time is complete, allow the pressure to release naturally for 5 minutes, then quick release any remaining pressure. Allow the cake to cool in the pan on a wire rack for 5 minutes. Turn the cake out onto the wire rack and allow to cool for at least 15 minutes more. Serve warm.

TIP | To make the cake easier to remove from the Instant Pot after cooking, make a sling for your pan with foil (page 13).

For best results, use a food scale to accurately measure flours. If you do not have a food scale, gently spoon the flour into your measuring cup so as not to compact it. Inaccurately measuring flour can leave you with a hard and dense finished product.

NUTRITION PER SERVING:

Calories **337** • Total Fat **15.4g** • Total Carb **51g** • Fiber **4g** • Total Sugars **21g** • Protein **3g**

For-Charity Buttermilk Pancake Bites

PROGRAM
Pressure Cook (High)

RELEASE
Natural and Quick

Gluten-Free

All of the goodness of an old-fashioned fundraiser pancake breakfast is condensed into these fluffy little bites. Sweetened with all-natural coconut sugar and a drizzle of real maple syrup, they are sure to satisfy any sweet tooth.

Makes **4 pancake bites** Serving Size **2 pancake bites** Prep Time **5 mins** Pressure Time **7 mins** Total Time **32 mins**

2 tsp salted butter, melted

⅓ cup buttermilk

1 large egg white

½ tsp pure vanilla extract

⅓ cup (43g) cassava flour

2 tsp coconut sugar

¼ tsp baking soda

¼ tsp salt

4 tsp pure maple syrup

1. In a small bowl, whisk together the butter, buttermilk, egg white, and vanilla. In a separate small bowl, stir together the cassava flour, coconut sugar, baking soda, and salt. Gently stir the flour mixture into the buttermilk mixture until just combined.

2. Spray 4 (4fl oz; 120ml) canning jars with nonstick spray, and pour the batter evenly into each. Drizzle 1 teaspoon maple syrup over each pancake bite.

3. Place the steam rack in the inner pot and add 1 cup water. Place the jars on the steam rack and rest the flat canning lid on top of each to keep out excess moisture. (There is no need to screw on the ring.)

4. Lock the lid and set the steam release valve to the sealing position. Select **Pressure Cook (High),** and set the cook time for **7 minutes.**

5. Once the cook time is complete, allow the pressure to release naturally for 5 minutes, then quick release any remaining pressure. Allow the pancake bites to cool, uncovered, in the jars on a wire rack for 10 minutes. Run a butter knife around the inside edges of the jars to make them easier to remove. Serve immediately.

TIP | For blueberry pancake bites, fold 1 tablespoon wild blueberries into the batter. Try finely chopped bananas and walnuts for a banana-nut version.

For best results, use a food scale to accurately measure flours. If you do not have a food scale, gently spoon the flour into your measuring cup so as not to compact it. Inaccurately measuring flour can leave you with a hard and dense finished product.

NUTRITION PER SERVING:
Calories **180** • Total Fat **4.3g** • Total Carb **33g** • Fiber **2g** • Total Sugars **14g** • Protein **4g**

Poached Salmon and Eggs with Yogurt Sauce

PROGRAM
Pressure Cook (Low)

RELEASE
Quick

Gluten-Free, Keto Friendly

This high-protein, low-carb breakfast is indulgent and has a flair of gourmet, but you'll be thrilled to find how quickly and easily this tangy and flavorful dish comes together in the Instant Pot!

Serves **2**   Serving Size **1 poached egg, 1 salmon fillet, and about ¼ cup sauce**   Prep Time **10 mins**   Pressure Time **5 mins**   Total Time **30 mins**

2 boneless, skinless salmon fillets, about 6oz (170g) each

½ small red onion, roughly chopped

2 tbsp roughly chopped dill

½ medium lemon, sliced into rounds

1 cup vegetable broth

2 large eggs

For the yogurt sauce:

⅓ cup plain full-fat Greek yogurt

2 tsp lemon juice

1 tbsp minced red onion

2 tsp finely chopped dill

⅛ tsp garlic powder

¼ tsp salt

⅛ tsp black pepper

1. Place the salmon fillets on the bottom of the inner pot in a single layer. Scatter the onion, dill, and lemon slices over the salmon, and pour in the vegetable broth.

2. Spray 2 wells of a small silicone egg bite mold (with four egg bite wells) with nonstick spray. Pour 1 tablespoon water into the same 2 wells. Crack an egg into each of the wells with the water.

3. Place an egg steamer trivet with 1½- to 2-inch (3.75–5cm) legs in the inner pot and place the silicone egg bite mold, uncovered, on the trivet above the salmon. Lock the lid and set the steam release valve to the sealing position. Select **Pressure Cook (Low),** and set the cook time for **5 minutes.**

4. While the salmon and eggs are cooking, make the yogurt sauce. In a small bowl, whisk together the Greek yogurt, lemon juice, onion, dill, garlic powder, salt, and pepper. Set aside until ready to serve.

5. Once the cook time is complete, quick release the pressure. With potholders, carefully remove the egg bite mold from the inner pot and pour off the excess water from the top of the eggs.

6. Using tongs or a spatula, carefully remove the salmon fillets from the inner pot and place on serving plates. Scoop the eggs out of the egg bite mold with a spoon, and place one alongside each salmon fillet. Top the salmon and eggs with the yogurt sauce, and serve immediately.

TIP | If you prefer very runny poached eggs, reduce the cook time to 4 minutes. If you prefer firmer eggs, increase the cook time to 6 minutes.

The eggs will continue to cook after they are taken out of the inner pot. Serve as quickly as possible after cooking.

NUTRITION PER SERVING:
Calories **471** • Total Fat **28.3g** • Total Carb **7g** • Fiber **1g** • Total Sugars **3g** • Protein **45g**

Sweet Potato Breakfast Egg Cups

This simple recipe is a perfect way to keep you from the drive-through on a busy weekday morning. Make a batch the night before, then in the morning, just reheat for a few seconds and enjoy!

PROGRAM
Pressure Cook (High)

RELEASE
Quick

Gluten-Free, Keto-Friendly Variation

Makes **2 egg cups**   Serving Size **1 egg cup**   Prep Time **10 mins**   Pressure Time **14 mins**   Total Time **35 mins**

¾ cup (about 3.5oz; 100g) peeled sweet potato cubes (½in; 1.25cm pieces)

¼ cup diced ham

2 tbsp shredded Cheddar cheese

2 large eggs

Salt, to taste

Black pepper, to taste

Finely chopped chives, for garnish

1. Place a steamer basket with feet in the inner pot and add 1 cup water. Add the sweet potato cubes to the steamer basket. Lock the lid and set the steam release valve to the sealing position. Select **Pressure Cook (High),** and set the cook time for **2 minutes.**

2. Once the cook time is complete, quick release the pressure and remove the steamer basket. Do not discard the water from the bottom of the inner pot. Press **Cancel.**

3. Spray 2 (8fl oz; 235ml) wide-mouth canning jars with nonstick spray. To each jar, layer ½ of the sweet potato cubes, 2 tablespoons ham, and 1 tablespoon Cheddar.

4. Pour 1 lightly beaten egg into each jar. Season with salt and pepper to taste.

5. Place the steam rack in the inner pot, and place the jars on the steam rack. Lock the lid and set the steam release valve to the sealing position. Select **Pressure Cook (High),** and set the cook time for **12 minutes.**

6. Once the cook time is complete, quick release the pressure. Allow the egg cups to cool on a wire rack for 5 minutes. Garnish with chopped chives and serve immediately.

TIP | Make it keto friendly: Use cooked cauliflower or spaghetti squash in place of the sweet potato to reduce the carb load. Skip to Step 3.

This recipe is easy to customize. Try bacon or sausage instead of ham, or use different varieties of cheese to mix things up.

Use up leftover baked or roasted sweet potatoes. Cut the already cooked sweet potatoes into ½-inch (1.25cm) cubes, and skip to Step 3.

NUTRITION PER SERVING:
Calories **168** • Total Fat **8.2g** • Total Carb **9g** • Fiber **1g** • Total Sugars **2g** • Protein **14g**

Spinach Prosciutto Egg Bites

PROGRAM
Pressure Cook (High)

RELEASE
Natural and Quick

**Gluten-Free,
Keto Friendly**

These egg bites are blended before cooking, which makes them velvety smooth and creamy. The Gouda and prosciutto provide savory and smoky flavors, and all of the protein in these little bites is sure to satisfy the appetite for hours.

Makes **4 egg bites** Serving Size **2 egg bites** Prep Time **10 mins** Pressure Time **9 mins** Total Time **40 mins**

2 large eggs

¼ cup 4% milkfat cottage cheese

⅛ tsp salt

1oz (25g) finely cubed smoked Gouda cheese (about ¼ cup)

1oz (25g) prosciutto, roughly chopped

¼ cup chopped fresh spinach (loosely packed)

1. In a blender, add the eggs, cottage cheese, and salt. Blend until smooth. Add the Gouda, prosciutto, and spinach, and pulse until they are very finely chopped but not fully puréed.

2. Spray a small silicone egg bite mold (with four egg bite wells) with nonstick spray. Divide the egg mixture between the four wells.

3. Place the steam rack in the inner pot and add 1 cup water. Place the silicone mold, uncovered, on top of the steam rack. Lock the lid and set the steam release valve to the sealing position. Select **Pressure Cook (High),** and set the cook time for **9 minutes.**

4. Once the cook time is complete, allow the pressure to release naturally for 5 minutes, then quick release any remaining pressure.

5. Allow the egg bites to cool in the mold on a wire rack for 5 minutes. Invert the mold onto a paper towel–lined plate to absorb any liquid. Serve immediately.

TIP Smoked Gouda adds a delicious flavor to these bites, but if it is too difficult to locate, regular Gouda can be substituted.

These little bites reheat wonderfully. Make a double batch and store in the refrigerator for a quick breakfast on a weekday morning.

Customize by substituting different varieties of cheese, breakfast meats, and greens. Try bacon, Cheddar cheese, and collard greens; or ham, Swiss cheese, and kale!

NUTRITION PER SERVING:

Calories **210** • Total Fat **15.1g** • Total Carb **2g** • Fiber **0g** • Total Sugars **1g** • Protein **16g**

Easy-Peel Hard-Boiled Eggs

Boiled eggs are practically the definition of a healthy breakfast, and the Instant Pot makes them easier than ever. Packed with protein and healthy fat, your appetite is sure to be satisfied with these simple additions to your breakfast plate.

PROGRAM
Pressure Cook (High)

RELEASE
Quick

Gluten-Free, Dairy-Free, Keto Friendly

Serves **2–6**   Serving Size **2 eggs**   Prep Time **1 min**   Pressure Time **6 mins**   Total Time **17 mins**

4–12 eggs

1. Place a steamer basket with feet in the inner pot and add 1 cup water. Add the desired number of eggs to the steamer basket.

2. Lock the lid and set the steam release valve to the sealing position. Select **Pressure Cook (High),** and set the cook time for **6 minutes.**

3. Once the cook time is complete, quick release the pressure. Immediately transfer the eggs to a large bowl of ice water. Allow the eggs cool completely—this takes about 5 minutes. Drain the water and ice, peel away the eggshells, and serve immediately. Store any leftovers in the fridge for easy snacks throughout the day.

TIP Reduce the cook time to 3 minutes for soft-boiled eggs, and serve immediately after a 1-minute plunge into the ice water.

If you don't have a steamer basket, you can use the steaming rack that comes with the Instant Pot—you just might have to do a little stacking to make sure all the eggs are sitting above the water and not directly on the bottom of the inner pot.

NUTRITION PER SERVING:

Calories **143** • Total Fat **9.5g** • Total Carb **1g** • Fiber **0g** • Total Sugars **0g** • Protein **13g**

Entrées, Soups, and Stews

Greek Chicken Gyro Bowls

PROGRAM
Pressure Cook (High)

RELEASE
Natural and Quick

Gluten-Free, Keto-Friendly Variation

This recipe is a little involved, but after one taste you'll see that it's worth the extra effort! Filled with mouthwatering Greek chicken, marinated onions, feta cheese, and more, the flavor combination in these bowls is pretty close to perfection.

Serves **2**   Serving Size **1 gyro bowl**   Prep Time **30 mins**   Pressure Time **4 mins**   Total Time **55 mins**

½ small red onion, thinly sliced

2 boneless, skinless chicken thighs, about 4oz (110g) each

½ cup white jasmine rice, rinsed

½ cup water

4 small lemon slices

½ medium tomato

1 small cucumber

¼ cup pitted kalamata olives

¼ cup feta cheese crumbles

For the marinade:

2 tbsp olive oil

3 tbsp balsamic vinegar

2 cloves garlic, finely minced

1 tsp chopped fresh oregano

½ tsp salt

¼ tsp black pepper

⅛ tsp red pepper flakes

For the tzatziki:

¼ cup plain full-fat Greek yogurt

2 tbsp minced, peeled cucumber

2 tsp finely chopped dill

1 tsp finely chopped oregano

1 small clove garlic, minced

Zest of ½ small lemon

⅛ tsp salt

Dash of black pepper

1. Prepare the marinade. In a small bowl, whisk together the olive oil, balsamic vinegar, garlic, oregano, salt, pepper, and red pepper flakes.

2. To another small bowl, add the red onion rings. Drizzle with half of the marinade, and toss to coat. Cover and refrigerate.

3. To the remaining marinade, add the chicken thighs, and turn to coat. Set aside to marinate for 20 minutes at room temperature.

4. While the chicken is marinating, make the tzatziki sauce. In a small bowl, stir together the yogurt, cucumber, dill, oregano, garlic, lemon zest, salt, and pepper. Cover and refrigerate.

5. Once the chicken has marinated for 20 minutes, add the rice and ½ cup water to the inner pot. Lay the marinated chicken thighs on top of the rice, and place two lemon slices on each thigh. Lock the lid and set the steam release valve to the sealing position. Select **Pressure Cook (High)**, and set the cook time for **4 minutes.**

6. While the chicken and rice are cooking, dice the tomato and slice the cucumber. Halve the olives, if desired. Set aside.

7. Once the cook time is complete, allow the pressure to release naturally for 5 minutes, then quick release any remaining pressure.

8. Remove the chicken thighs from the inner pot and slice into strips. Portion the rice into two serving bowls, and top each bowl with the chicken, tomatoes, cucumbers, olives, feta, and marinated onions. Garnish with the cooked lemon slices, if desired, and serve immediately with the tzatziki on the side.

TIP Make it keto friendly: You can drastically cut the carbs in this meal by making it into a salad instead of a rice bowl. Cook the chicken as directed in ½ cup water, omitting the jasmine rice. Serve over a bed of lettuce.

NUTRITION PER SERVING:
Calories **503** • Total Fat **21.1g** • Total Carb **56g** • Fiber **3g** • Total Sugars **7g** • Protein **20g**

Chicken Bone Broth

This simple and frugal recipe is the unsung hero in countless dishes. It not only provides a medley of savory flavors to soups and stews, but it also offers collagen and a multitude of nutrients that are essential for health.

PROGRAM
Soup/Broth (High)

RELEASE
Natural and Quick

Gluten-Free, Dairy-Free, Keto Friendly

Makes **5 cups**   Serving Size **1 cup**   Prep Time **5 mins**   Pressure Time **2 hours**   Total Time **3 hours**

1 chicken carcass, picked clean (from Rotisserie-Style Chicken and Lemony Rice on page 46)

1 stalk celery, roughly chopped

1 carrot, roughly chopped

½ small onion, roughly chopped

1 tsp salt

¼ tsp black pepper

1 tbsp apple cider vinegar

5 cups water

1. To the inner pot, add the chicken carcass, celery, carrot, onion, salt, pepper, and apple cider vinegar. Cover with 5 cups water.

2. Lock the lid and set the steam release valve to the sealing position. Select **Soup/Broth (High),** and set the cook time for **2 hours.**

3. Once the cook time is complete, allow the pressure to release naturally for 20 minutes, then quick release any remaining pressure. Use a fine-mesh strainer to strain out the bones and vegetables, and discard. Pour the broth into glass jars and allow to cool slightly before transferring to the refrigerator for storage.

4. Chill the broth in the refrigerator overnight. When the fat layer at the top has hardened, remove and discard, leaving just the bone broth.

5. To enjoy, sip the warmed broth from a mug, or use in any recipe calling for chicken broth or stock. Use or freeze within 4 days.

TIP | Freeze extra broth in ice cube trays, then transfer the frozen cubes to a freezer-safe container. Easily use the preportioned cubes in recipes. Eight regular-size cubes usually equal about 1 cup broth.

Cook rice in bone broth instead of water as a great way to get the nutritional benefits of the broth as well as a delicious, savory rice dish.

Make beef bone broth by substituting one or two beef soup bones for the chicken carcass. Roasting the beef bones before pressure cooking gives the broth a deep, rich flavor.

NUTRITION PER SERVING:
Calories **50** • Total Fat **1g** • Total Carb **0g** • Fiber **0g** • Total Sugars **<1g** • Protein **10g**

Layered Chicken Enchilada Casserole

PROGRAM
Pressure Cook (High)

RELEASE
Natural and Quick

Gluten-Free

So many flavors and textures come together in this tasty Mexican dish. The prep time for this casserole is super quick, and the Instant Pot does all the hard work. You can start it, forget it, and before you know it, dinner is ready!

Serves **4**   Serving Size **¼ of the pan**   Prep Time **10 mins**   Pressure Time **35 mins**   Total Time **1 hour 15 mins**

3 corn tortillas

1½ cups cooked and chopped chicken (such as leftovers from Rotisserie-Style Chicken and Lemony Rice on page 46), divided

½ cup No-Fuss Black Beans (page 109) or canned black beans, rinsed and drained, divided

½ cup corn kernels (fresh, frozen, or canned and drained), divided

¾ cup canned enchilada sauce, divided

6 tbsp shredded Cheddar cheese, divided

Sour cream (optional), for serving

Chopped scallions (optional), for serving

1. Spray a 1-quart (1l), oven-safe, flat-bottomed pan or baking dish with nonstick spray.

2. Layer the ingredients in the pan as follows: 1 tortilla (trimmed as necessary to fit in the pan), ¾ cup chicken, ¼ cup black beans, ¼ cup corn kernels, ¼ cup enchilada sauce, and 2 tablespoons Cheddar. Repeat these layers once more.

3. Place the remaining tortilla on top of the casserole, and cover with the remaining ¼ cup enchilada sauce. Sprinkle with the remaining 2 tablespoons Cheddar. Cover the bowl or pan tightly with foil.

4. Place the steam rack in the inner pot and add 1 cup water. Place the pan on the steam rack. Lock the lid and set the steam release valve to the sealing position. Select **Pressure Cook (High),** and set the cook time for **35 minutes.**

5. Once the cook time is complete, allow the pressure to release naturally for 5 minutes, then quick release any remaining pressure.

6. Remove the casserole from the inner pot and allow to cool for 10 minutes. Cut into fourths and serve with sour cream and chopped scallions, if desired.

TIP | This casserole is a great way to use up any leftovers you might have sitting in your refrigerator. Use leftover pinto beans or refried beans in place of the black beans, or use leftover ground beef or pulled pork in place of the chicken.

To make the dish easier to remove from the Instant Pot after cooking, make a sling for your pan with foil (page 13).

NUTRITION PER SERVING (EXCLUDING OPTIONS FOR SERVING):
Calories **291** • Total Fat **6g** • Total Carb **27g** • Fiber **3g** • Total Sugars **1g** • Protein **24g**

Rotisserie-Style Chicken and Lemony Rice

PROGRAM
Pressure Cook (High)

RELEASE
Natural and Quick

**Gluten-Free,
Dairy-Free**

It might surprise you to find out that you can cook a whole chicken in the Instant Pot Mini! This chicken cooks up beautifully, and the fragrant jasmine rice soaks up every last drop of the succulent flavor.

Serves **4**   Serving Size **1 chicken quarter and ½ cup rice**   Prep Time **5 mins**   Pressure Time **30 mins**   Total Time **1 hour 16 mins**

2 tbsp fresh lemon juice

½ cup water

½ tsp dried thyme leaves

½ tsp garlic powder

1 tsp onion powder

½ tsp smoked paprika

½ tsp black pepper

2 tsp salt

3–4lb (1.5kg–2kg) whole chicken

¾ cup white jasmine rice

1. Add the lemon juice and ½ cup water to the inner pot. In a small bowl, stir together the thyme, garlic powder, onion powder, paprika, pepper, and salt. Rub the spice mixture all over the outside and inside of the chicken. Place the chicken in the inner pot.

2. Lock the lid and set the steam release valve to the sealing position. Select **Pressure Cook (High),** and set the cook time for **6 minutes per pound of chicken.** This equals **18 minutes** for a 3-pound (1.5kg) chicken or **24 minutes** for a 4-pound (2kg) chicken.

3. Once the cook time is complete, allow the pressure to release naturally for 5 minutes, then quick release any remaining pressure. With tongs, carefully remove the chicken from the inner pot to a serving platter. Tent the chicken with foil and allow to rest while the rice cooks.

4. Strain the liquid that is left in the bottom of the inner pot to remove any bone fragments. Return 1¼ cups liquid to the inner pot. If you do not have enough liquid from the chicken, add some water. Stir in the jasmine rice. Lock the lid and set the steam release valve to the sealing position. Select **Pressure Cook (High),** and set the cook time for **6 minutes.**

5. Once the cook time is complete, allow the pressure to release naturally for 5 minutes, then quick release any remaining pressure. Fluff the rice with a fork and serve immediately with the chicken.

TIP   If you're cooking for two, you can use the leftovers to make Layered Chicken Enchilada Casserole (page 45) or Nourishing Chicken Noodle Soup (page 84).

Save the bones and carcass after they've been picked clean and use them to make a batch of Chicken Bone Broth (page 44).

Check the organic section for a chicken that is 4 pounds (2kg) or less. Organic chickens tend to be on the smaller side when compared to conventionally raised chickens.

NUTRITION PER SERVING (WITH A 4LB; 2KG CHICKEN):
Calories **368** • Total Fat **6.4g** • Total Carb **29g** • Fiber **1g** • Total Sugars **0g** • Protein **45g**

Taco Meatloaf Cups

These hearty meatloaf cups are high in protein and very low in carbs. This makes them very filling and sure to satisfy your hunger for hours. Dress them up with whatever toppings you enjoy on your tacos.

PROGRAM
Pressure Cook (High)

RELEASE
Natural and Quick

**Gluten-Free,
Keto Friendly**

Makes **2 meatloaf cups**   Serving Size **1 meatloaf cup**   Prep Time **10 mins**   Pressure Time **25 mins**   Total Time **55 mins**

10oz (285g) 90% lean ground beef

1 large egg

2 tbsp blanched almond flour

1 tsp chili powder

¼ tsp garlic powder

¼ tsp onion powder

¼ tsp ground cumin

½ tsp salt

¼ tsp black pepper

4 tbsp shredded Cheddar cheese, divided

For topping:
Chopped scallions

2 tbsp sliced black olives

2 tbsp salsa

2 tbsp sour cream

1. In a medium bowl, use your hands to mix together the ground beef, egg, almond flour, chili powder, garlic powder, onion powder, cumin, salt, pepper, and 2 tablespoons Cheddar.

2. Spray 2 (8fl oz; 235ml) wide-mouth canning jars with nonstick spray, and add half of the meatloaf mixture into each. Sprinkle the remaining 2 tablespoons Cheddar over the meatloaves.

3. Place the steam rack in the inner pot and add 1 cup water. Place the jars on the steam rack and rest the flat canning lid on top of each to keep out excess moisture. (There is no need to screw on the ring.) Lock the lid and set the steam release valve to the sealing position. Select **Pressure Cook (High),** and set the cook time for **25 minutes.**

4. Once the cook time is complete, allow the pressure to release naturally for 5 minutes, then quick release any remaining pressure. Allow the meatloaf cups to cool uncovered in the jars for 5 minutes. Run a butter knife around the inside edges of the jars to make them easier to remove. Remove the meatloaves from the jars and transfer to a serving tray. Discard any excess drippings left in the bottom of the jars.

5. Top the meatloaves with scallions, black olives, salsa, and sour cream, and serve immediately.

TIP | These mini meatloaves are wonderful served alongside rice and beans. Keep the whole meal low in carbs by serving atop a green salad.

For a variation, try these meatloaves with 90% lean ground turkey instead of beef.

NUTRITION PER SERVING:
Calories **425** • Total Fat **27.5g** • Total Carb **5g** • Fiber **1g** • Total Sugars **2g** • Protein **37g**

Asian Chicken Lettuce Wraps

PROGRAM
Sauté (More)

RELEASE
None

**Gluten-Free,
Dairy-Free**

These delicate chicken bundles are full of vegetables and so refreshing. Restaurant versions of this dish are usually served with deep-fried noodles, but this recipe relies on a fresher option for its crunch: crisp bean sprouts and roasted cashews.

Serves **2**   Serving Size **about ¾ cup filling and 2–3 lettuce leaves**   Prep Time **15 mins**   Pressure Time **0 mins**   Total Time **25 mins**

1 batch Sweet Chili Sauce (page 125; optional)

2 scallions, divided

1 tbsp avocado oil or olive oil

8oz (225g) ground chicken

½ cup shredded carrots

2 tbsp chopped, roasted, and salted cashews

Chopped cilantro, for garnish

Toasted sesame seeds, for garnish

4–6 romaine lettuce leaves

¾ cup roughly chopped fresh bean sprouts

For the sauce mixture:

1 tbsp honey

2 tbsp tamari

1 tbsp rice vinegar

2 tsp Sriracha sauce

½ tsp arrowroot starch, or cornstarch

1. Pour the Sweet Chili Sauce into a small serving dish, if using, and set aside. Chop the white portions of the scallions, and set aside. Finely chop the green portions of the scallions, and set aside for garnish.

2. Select **Sauté (More),** and add the oil to the inner pot. Once hot, add the ground chicken and sauté for 6 minutes, or until the meat is cooked through.

3. While the chicken is cooking, make the sauce mixture. In a small bowl, whisk together the honey, tamari, rice vinegar, Sriracha, and starch.

4. To the chicken in the inner pot, add the shredded carrots and the chopped white portions of the scallions. Sauté for 1 minute more. Add the sauce mixture. Stir and simmer until the sauce has thickened, about 1 minute. Press **Cancel** to turn off Keep Warm. Remove the inner pot from the base, and stir in the cashews.

5. Transfer the chicken filling to a serving bowl. Garnish with cilantro, sesame seeds, and the green portions of the scallions. Serve immediately on a platter alongside the lettuce leaves, bean sprouts, and Sweet Chili Sauce. To assemble each wrap, fill a lettuce leaf with a scoop of the chicken filling, sprinkle with bean sprouts, and drizzle with Sweet Chili Sauce, if desired.

TIP | This recipe cooks up in a snap. It's so quick that you won't even need to use the Pressure Cook setting on your Instant Pot.

NUTRITION PER SERVING (EXCLUDING GARNISHES):
Calories **384** • Total Fat **13.4g** • Total Carb **33g** • Fiber **3g** • Total Sugars **22g** • Protein **34g**

Lime-Cilantro Pulled Pork

You can't go wrong with the tangy and flavorful combination of fresh lime and cilantro. This pulled pork cooks to a fall-apart perfection and makes a wonderful filling for tacos and burritos or a topping for taco salad.

PROGRAM
**Sauté (More),
Pressure Cook (High)**

RELEASE
Natural and Quick

Gluten-Free, Dairy-Free, Keto Friendly

Serves **4**　　　Serving Size **about ½ cup**　　　Prep Time **15 mins**　　　Pressure Time **40 mins**　　　Total Time **1 hour 20 mins**

1lb (450g) boneless pork shoulder, fat trimmed, cut into quarters

1 tsp salt

½ tsp black pepper

1 tsp avocado oil or olive oil

¼ cup water

1 tsp chili powder

¼ tsp garlic powder

¼ tsp onion powder

Juice of 2 limes, divided

3 tbsp chopped cilantro, divided

1. Season the quarters of pork shoulder on all sides with the salt and pepper. Select **Sauté (More)** and add the oil to the inner pot. When hot, sear the pieces of pork for 4 minutes on each side. Press **Cancel.**

2. Add ¼ cup water, chili powder, garlic powder, onion powder, juice of 1 lime, and 2 tablespoons chopped cilantro. Lock the lid and set the steam release valve to the sealing position. Select **Pressure Cook (High),** and set the cook time for **40 minutes.**

3. Once the cook time is complete, allow the pressure to release naturally for 5 minutes, then quick release any remaining pressure.

4. Press **Cancel** and select **Sauté (More).** Using two forks, shred the pork in the inner pot while bringing up to a simmer. Allow to simmer for 5 minutes, or until the liquid is reduced by about half.

5. Top the pork with the juice of the remaining lime and the remaining 1 tablespoon chopped cilantro. Serve immediately.

TIP | For a variation, make this recipe with chicken breast or thigh meat instead of pork.

NUTRITION PER SERVING:
Calories **165** • Total Fat **7.7g** • Total Carb **2g** • Fiber **0g** • Total Sugars **0g** • Protein **21g**

Asian Plum Short Ribs

These fall-off-the-bone ribs beautifully balance sweet, salty, and umami flavors, and they pair deliciously with freshly cooked cauliflower rice. Pressure cooking meat on the bone also releases a whole host of nutrients and collagen into your meal.

PROGRAM
Pressure Cook (High), Sauté (More)

RELEASE
Natural and Quick

Gluten-Free, Dairy-Free

Serves **2**   Serving Size **2 short ribs**   Prep Time **35 mins**   Pressure Time **46 mins**   Total Time **2 hours 40 mins**

1 tsp avocado oil or olive oil

4 bone-in beef short ribs (about 1½lbs; 680g)

½ tsp salt

¼ tsp black pepper

¼ cup beef broth or water

½ cup Asian Plum Sauce

1 scallion, finely chopped, for garnish

Toasted sesame seeds, for garnish

For the Asian Plum Sauce:

½ cup prunes

¼ cup tamari

¼ cup water

1 tsp ginger powder

1 tbsp fish sauce

¼ tsp red pepper flakes

2 tbsp rice vinegar

1 star anise pod

¼ cup coconut sugar

1. Make the plum sauce. In the inner pot, stir together the prunes, tamari, ¼ cup water, ginger powder, fish sauce, red pepper flakes, rice vinegar, and star anise pod. Lock the lid and set the steam release valve to the sealing position. Select **Pressure Cook (High),** and set the cook time for **6 minutes.**

2. Once the cook time is complete, allow the pressure to release naturally for 5 minutes, then quick release any remaining pressure. Press **Cancel** to turn off Keep Warm.

3. Remove and discard the star anise pod. Stir in the coconut sugar. Using a stand blender or immersion blender, blend the mixture until smooth.

4. Select **Sauté (More),** and add the oil to the inner pot. Season the short ribs with the salt and pepper. Once the pot is hot, working in batches, add the short ribs and sear for 4 minutes on each side. If the ribs stick when attempting to turn, allow them to sear for another 1 to 2 minutes until they release easily.

5. Add the broth or water to the inner pot and spoon the plum sauce evenly over the short ribs. Do not stir. Press **Cancel** to turn off Sauté. Lock the lid and set the steam release valve to the sealing position. Select **Pressure Cook (High),** and set the cook time for **40 minutes.**

6. Once the cook time is complete, allow the pressure to release naturally for 5 minutes, then quick release any remaining pressure.

7. Place the short ribs in a serving dish. Spoon a bit of the remaining Asian Plum Sauce over the ribs and sprinkle with the scallion and toasted sesame seeds. Serve immediately. Store any leftover plum sauce in an airtight container in the refrigerator for up to 2 weeks.

TIP | The plum sauce makes a delicious dipping or finishing sauce for many dishes. Use as a dipping sauce for wontons and dumplings or as a topping for lettuce wraps and stir-fry dishes.

Take a shortcut by using store-bought plum sauce.

NUTRITION PER SERVING (¼ CUP ASIAN PLUM SAUCE PER SERVING):
Calories **535** • Total Fat **28g** • Total Carb **24g** • Fiber **1g** • Total Sugars **23g** • Protein **46g**

Cranberry Chicken

Don't worry if fresh cranberries aren't currently in season because this recipe works just as well with frozen ones. Any time of year is a good time to enjoy this sweet and tangy, melt-in-your-mouth chicken dish.

PROGRAM
**Sauté (More),
Pressure Cook (High)**

RELEASE
Natural and Quick

**Gluten-Free,
Dairy-Free**

Serves **2**   Serving Size **about ¾ cup chicken and sauce**   Prep Time **35 mins**   Pressure Time **10 mins**   Total Time **1 hour 20 mins**

1 tbsp avocado oil or olive oil

2 boneless, skinless chicken thighs, about 6oz (170g) each, quartered

½ cup sliced yellow onion (2in; 5cm long)

¼ tsp salt

1 tbsp tamari

¼ cup water

1 cinnamon stick

1 star anise pod

1 cup cranberries (fresh or frozen)

Zest and juice of 1 small orange

¼ cup plus 2 tbsp honey

1 batch Pot-in-Pot White Rice (page 94; optional)

1. Select **Sauté (More),** and add the oil to the inner pot. When hot, add the chicken and onion. Sprinkle with the salt. Sauté, stirring occasionally, for 6 minutes, or until the chicken is no longer pink.

2. Press **Cancel,** and stir in the tamari and ¼ cup water. Scatter the cinnamon stick, star anise pod, and cranberries over the chicken. Add the orange juice and zest, and drizzle the honey over the top, but do not stir.

3. If cooking Pot-in-Pot White rice, add the egg steamer trivet with 1½–2-inch (3.75–5cm) legs to the inner pot. Place the pan of white rice, water, and salt on the trivet above the chicken mixture. (See page 94 for the complete recipe.)

4. Lock the lid and set the steam release valve to the sealing position. Select **Pressure Cook (High),** and set the cook time for **10 minutes.**

5. Once the cook time is complete, allow the pressure to release naturally for 5 minutes, then quick release any remaining pressure. Press **Cancel** and select **Sauté (More).** Bring the pot up to a simmer and allow to cook, stirring occasionally, for 6 to 8 minutes, or until the sauce has reduced by about half. Serve immediately over rice, if using.

TIP | Sugars like honey have a tendency to scorch on the bottom of the Instant Pot. To avoid this, the honey is drizzled over the top of the chicken mixture and not stirred into the sauce before pressure cooking.

Try this recipe over mashed sweet potato for a delicious harvest-time meal.

NUTRITION PER SERVING (EXCLUDING RICE):
Calories **505** • Total Fat **14.1g** • Total Carb **63g** • Fiber **3g** • Total Sugars **56g** • Protein **35g**

Cinnamon Apple Pork Tenderloin

Apples and cinnamon add wonderful spice and sweetness to this pork dish. An ultraquick 1-minute cook time is enough to cook this tenderloin through while still keeping it perfectly moist and tender.

PROGRAM
**Sauté (More),
Pressure Cook (High)**

RELEASE
Natural and Quick

**Gluten-Free,
Dairy-Free**

Serves **4**   Serving Size **4 slices tenderloin and about ⅓ cup apple topping**   Prep Time **15 mins**   Pressure Time **1 min**   Total Time **35 mins**

1 tsp avocado oil or olive oil

1lb (450g) pork tenderloin, about 3in (7.5cm) in diameter at the thickest part

1 tsp salt

¼ tsp black pepper

¼ cup apple cider or apple juice

1 Fuji apple (or another sweet variety), unpeeled, cored, and cut into ½in (1.25cm) chunks

½ tsp ground cinnamon

¼ tsp garlic powder

¼ tsp onion powder

1 tsp arrowroot starch, or cornstarch

1 tbsp water

1. Select **Sauté (More)** and add the oil to the inner pot. Season the tenderloin with the salt and pepper. Once the pot is hot, add the tenderloin and sear for 4 minutes on each side.

2. Press **Cancel** and add the apple cider or apple juice. Scatter the apple pieces around the tenderloin, and sprinkle with the cinnamon, garlic powder, and onion powder.

3. Lock the lid and set the steam release valve to the sealing position. Select **Pressure Cook (High),** and set the cook time for **1 minute.**

4. Once the cook time is complete, allow the pressure to release naturally for 5 minutes, then quick release any remaining pressure.

5. Press **Cancel** and move the tenderloin to a cutting board to rest, uncovered, for 10 minutes.

6. Meanwhile, select **Sauté (More)** and bring the apple mixture up to a simmer. In a small bowl, combine the starch and 1 tablespoon water and stir into the inner pot. Simmer until the apple mixture has thickened, about 1 minute, and remove the inner pot from the base.

7. When the tenderloin has rested for 10 minutes, cut into 16 slices and transfer to a serving dish. Top the tenderloin with the apple mixture and serve immediately.

TIP | Cook time is dependent on the thickness of the tenderloin. A 1-pound (450g) tenderloin will typically be around 3 inches (7.5cm) in diameter at the thickest part. If you use a tenderloin that is thicker, increase the cook time to 3 minutes.

NUTRITION PER SERVING:
Calories **187** • Total Fat **5.2g** • Total Carb **9g** • Fiber **1g** • Total Sugars **7g** • Protein **23g**

Bacon and Mushroom Covered–Pork Chops

PROGRAM
**Sauté (More),
Pressure Cook (High)**

RELEASE
Natural and Quick

Gluten-Free, Dairy-Free, Keto Friendly

Mushrooms and bacon are powerful sources of umami and take these chops to the next level. They pair with rice or potatoes, or alongside cauliflower rice or spaghetti squash to keep it low carb.

Serves **2**   Serving Size **1 covered pork chop**   Prep Time **25 mins**   Pressure Time **12 mins**   Total Time **55 mins**

2 slices uncooked bacon, chopped

2 boneless pork-sirloin chops, cut as needed to fit in the bottom of the inner pot, about 5oz (140g) each

½ tsp salt

¼ tsp black pepper

4oz (110g) sliced cremini mushrooms (about 1½ cups)

2 tbsp vegetable broth or water

½ tsp dried thyme leaves

½ tsp garlic powder

1 tsp arrowroot starch, or cornstarch

1 tbsp water

1. Select **Sauté (More).** Add the bacon to the inner pot and cook until browned and crispy. Remove the bacon to a paper towel–lined plate, leaving the rendered bacon fat in the pot. Set aside the bacon crumbles.

2. Season the pork chops with salt and pepper, and sear in the inner pot for 3 minutes on each side. Remove the chops from the pot and press **Cancel** to turn off Sauté.

3. Add the mushrooms and broth or water to the inner pot, and place the pork chops on top. Sprinkle the pork chops and mushrooms with the thyme leaves and garlic powder. Select **Pressure Cook (High),** and set the cook time for **12 minutes.**

4. Once the cook time is complete, allow the pressure to release naturally for 5 minutes, then quick release any remaining pressure. Press **Cancel** to turn off Keep Warm.

5. Remove the pork chops to a serving dish. Select **Sauté (More).** In a small bowl, mix together the starch and 1 tablespoon water. Stir the mixture into the inner pot and simmer just until thickened, about 1 minute. Remove the inner pot from the base.

6. Top the pork chops in the serving dish with the mushrooms and sauce, and sprinkle with the bacon crumbles. Serve immediately.

TIP | This recipe is very low in carbs as written, but if you want to reduce the carbs even further, you can omit the arrowroot or cornstarch thickener at the end. Instead, thicken the sauce by selecting Sauté (More) after removing the cooked pork chops from the pot and simmering the sauce until reduced to the desired consistency.

NUTRITION PER SERVING:
Calories **238** • Total Fat **15.5g** • Total Carb **4g** • Fiber **1g** • Total Sugars **1g** • Protein **21g**

Buffalo Chicken–Stuffed Sweet Potatoes

This recipe offers a balance of energizing carbs, protein, and healthy fat, as well as perfectly balanced flavors and textures. Spicy buffalo chicken, tangy bleu cheese, creamy avocado, and crunchy red onions will have you loving this easy weeknight dinner.

PROGRAM
Pressure Cook (High), Sauté (More)

RELEASE
Natural and Quick

Gluten-Free, Keto-Friendly Variation

Makes **2 stuffed sweet potatoes** Serving Size **1 stuffed sweet potato** Prep Time **10 mins** Pressure Time **12 mins** Total Time **40 mins**

10oz (285g) chicken thigh meat, cut into 1-in (2.5cm) cubes

2 tbsp Frank's RedHot Sauce (reduce to 1 tbsp for a mild spice level)

1 tbsp salted butter

2 tsp Worcestershire sauce (gluten-free, if needed)

2 medium sweet potatoes, 2–2½in (5–6.25cm) in diameter and about 8oz (225g) each

For topping:
2 tbsp bleu cheese crumbles

1 tbsp finely chopped cilantro

1 tbsp finely chopped red onion

½ medium avocado, diced

1. In the inner pot, stir together the chicken, hot sauce, butter, and Worcestershire sauce. Place a tall egg steamer trivet with 2-inch (5cm) legs in the inner pot, and place the sweet potatoes on the rack above the chicken mixture.

2. Lock the lid and set the steam release valve to the sealing position. Select **Pressure Cook (High),** and set the cook time for **12 minutes.**

3. Once the cook time is complete, allow the pressure to release naturally for 5 minutes, then quick release any remaining pressure. Press **Cancel** to turn off Keep Warm. Using tongs, remove the sweet potatoes and the trivet from the inner pot.

4. Select **Sauté (More),** and allow the chicken to simmer, stirring often, for 5 minutes, or until the sauce has reduced by about half.

5. Slice lengthwise through the sweet potato skins, and using a kitchen towel or potholder, press the ends of the potatoes toward each other so the sweet potatoes pop open. Fluff the insides with a fork. Spoon half of the chicken mixture into each potato. Top with bleu cheese crumbles, cilantro, red onion, and avocado. Serve immediately.

TIP | The cook time needed for the sweet potatoes depends on their diameter at the widest part. For this recipe, choose sweet potatoes with a diameter of no more than 2½ inches (6.25cm). If your sweet potatoes are larger, increase the cook time by a few minutes.

Make it keto friendly: Cutting carbs? Try this recipe over cooked spaghetti squash (page 104) instead of sweet potatoes.

NUTRITION PER SERVING:
Calories **574** • Total Fat **24g** • Total Carb **52g** • Fiber **11g** • Total Sugars **5g** • Protein **40g**

German Sausage and Sauerkraut Dinner

In this dish, the tang of the sauerkraut, the grainy mustard, and the caraway seeds meld beautifully to make a hearty and flavorful dinner. This meal provides a great balance of starch and protein along with plenty of veggies!

PROGRAM
**Sauté (More),
Pressure Cook (High)**

RELEASE
Natural and Quick

**Gluten-Free,
Dairy-Free, Keto-
Friendly Variation**

Serves **2**   Serving Size **about 1¾ cups**   Prep Time **10 mins**   Pressure Time **2 mins**   Total Time **35 mins**

1 tsp avocado oil or olive oil

6oz (170g) precooked kielbasa, cut into 1in (2.5cm) chunks

1 cup sliced red onion

1 tbsp German-style whole-grain mustard

½ tsp whole caraway seeds

8oz (225g) cubed red potatoes (about 2 medium potatoes)

1 cup sauerkraut, undrained

2 tbsp chopped parsley

1. Select **Sauté (More),** and add the oil to the inner pot. When hot, add the kielbasa pieces and sear for 4 minutes on each side. Add the onion and sauté for 2 minutes more. Stir in the mustard and caraway seeds, and press **Cancel** to turn off Sauté.

2. Add the potatoes in a layer over the kielbasa and onion. Then add the sauerkraut in a layer over the potatoes. Do not stir. Lock the lid and set the steam release valve to the sealing position. Select **Pressure Cook (High),** and set the cook time for **2 minutes.**

3. Once the cook time is complete, allow the pressure to release naturally for 5 minutes, then quick release any remaining pressure. Stir in the parsley and serve immediately.

TIP | Make it keto friendly: Omit the potatoes and serve alongside an additional vegetable side dish.

NUTRITION PER SERVING:
Calories **420** • Total Fat **27.9g** • Total Carb **30g** • Fiber **5g** • Total Sugars **7g** • Protein **13g**

Tangy Beef and Broccoli

In this recipe, melt-in-your-mouth steak strips and perfectly tender broccoli are coated in a rich and tangy, slightly sweetened sauce. This is a great go-to when the craving for Chinese takeout hits.

PROGRAM
**Sauté (More),
Pressure Cook (High),
Pressure Cook (Low)**

RELEASE
Natural and Quick

**Gluten-Free,
Dairy-Free**

Serves **2**   Serving Size **about 1 cup**   Prep Time **35 mins**   Pressure Time **3 mins**   Total Time **1 hour**

1 tsp avocado oil or olive oil

8oz (225g) flank or skirt steak, sliced against the grain into thin strips

2 tbsp beef broth or water

6oz (170g) fresh broccoli florets (about 3 cups)

For the marinade:
1 tbsp tamari
1 tbsp rice vinegar
1 tbsp avocado oil or olive oil

For the sauce:
2 tbsp tamari
1 tbsp rice vinegar
1 tsp fish sauce
1 tsp toasted sesame oil
1 tbsp tomato paste
1 tbsp coconut sugar
¼ tsp red pepper flakes
¼ tsp ginger powder
1 small scallion, halved lengthwise and finely sliced
2 tsp arrowroot starch, or cornstarch

1. Prepare the marinade. In a medium bowl, stir together the tamari, rice vinegar, and oil. Stir in the steak strips and marinate for 20 minutes at room temperature.

2. While the steak is marinating, make the sauce. In a small bowl, whisk together the tamari, rice vinegar, fish sauce, sesame oil, tomato paste, coconut sugar, red pepper flakes, ginger powder, scallion, and starch. Set aside.

3. Select **Sauté (More),** and add the oil to the inner pot. When hot, add the steak and discard any remaining marinade. Sauté for 4 minutes, or until the steak is no longer pink. Add the broth or water. Press **Cancel** to turn off Sauté.

4. Lock the lid and set the steam release valve to the sealing position. Select **Pressure Cook (High),** and set the cook time for **3 minutes.**

5. Once the cook time is complete, allow the pressure to release naturally for 5 minutes, then quick release any remaining pressure. Press **Cancel** to turn off Keep Warm.

6. Stir in the broccoli florets. Lock the lid and set the steam release valve to the sealing position. Select **Pressure Cook (Low),** and set the cook time for **0 minutes.**

7. Once the cook time is complete, quick release the pressure. Press **Cancel** to turn off Keep Warm. Select **Sauté (More),** and add the sauce. Simmer for 1 minute to thicken, then remove the inner pot from the base. Serve immediately.

TIP | Vegetables can overcook easily under pressure. Adding them in at the very end and using a 0-minute cook time on low pressure is a great way to perfectly cook delicate vegetables without letting them turn to mush.

NUTRITION PER SERVING (USING FLANK STEAK AND BEEF BROTH):
Calories **308** • Total Fat **17.3g** • Total Carb **11g** • Fiber **1g** • Total Sugars **6g** • Protein **28g**

Orange Marmalade Chicken

PROGRAM
**Sauté (More),
Pressure Cook (High)**

RELEASE
Natural and Quick

**Gluten-Free,
Dairy-Free**

This sweet and sticky orange chicken will satisfy your takeout cravings without any MSG or a deep fryer. You can feel great about indulging in this made-from-scratch, high-protein dish!

Serves **2** Serving Size **1 cup** Prep Time **10 mins** Pressure Time **6 mins** Total Time **40 mins**

1 tsp avocado oil or olive oil

12oz (340g) chicken thigh meat, diced

3 tbsp tamari

2 tsp minced fresh ginger

¼ tsp garlic powder

¼ tsp onion powder

⅛ tsp red pepper flakes

1 tsp toasted sesame oil

⅓ cup Orange Marmalade (page 26)

1 tbsp tomato paste

1 batch Pot-in-Pot White Rice (page 94; optional)

1 tsp arrowroot starch, or cornstarch (optional for thickening)

1 tbsp water (only if using starch)

Toasted sesame seeds, for garnish

Chopped scallions, for garnish

1. Select **Sauté (More),** and add the oil to the inner pot. When hot, add the chicken. Sauté for 5 minutes, or until the chicken is no longer pink. Press **Cancel.**

2. Add the tamari, ginger, garlic powder, onion powder, red pepper flakes, and sesame oil. Stir to combine. Spoon the Orange Marmalade and tomato paste on top of the chicken mixture, but do not stir.

3. If cooking Pot-in-Pot White rice, add the egg steamer trivet with 1½–2-inch (3.75–5cm) legs to the inner pot. Place the pan of white rice, water, and salt on the trivet above the chicken mixture. (See page 94 for the complete recipe.)

4. Lock the lid and set the steam release valve to the sealing position. Select **Pressure Cook (High),** and set the cook time for **6 minutes.**

5. Once the cook time is complete, allow the pressure to release naturally for 5 minutes, then quick release any remaining pressure.

6. Remove the pan of rice and the egg steamer trivet (if applicable), and stir the chicken mixture. If the sauce needs thickening, select **Sauté (More).** In a small bowl, mix together the starch and 1 tablespoon water, and stir into the chicken mixture. Bring just up to a simmer to thicken, then remove the inner pot from the base.

7. Serve the chicken and sauce over the white rice, if desired, and top with a sprinkle of toasted sesame seeds and scallions.

TIP | Don't have time to make your own marmalade? Simplify by using store bought .

Sugar-containing jams and thick tomato products tend to scorch on the bottom of the Instant Pot. To avoid this, the marmalade and tomato paste are added on top of the chicken mixture but not stirred in until after cooking.

NUTRITION PER SERVING (EXCLUDING RICE):
Calories **574** • Total Fat **34.1g** • Total Carb **39g** • Fiber **1g** • Total Sugars **34g** • Protein **32g**

Zuppa Toscana One-Pot Pasta

This creamy sausage and kale pasta dish is a take on a delicious and classic Italian soup. Using chickpea pasta keeps this dish grain-free, and you'll be surprised to find that you can cook it from start to finish in about half an hour.

PROGRAM
**Sauté (More),
Pressure Cook (High)**

RELEASE
Quick

Gluten-Free, Dairy-Free Variation

Serves **2** Serving Size **about 2 cups** Prep Time **10 mins** Pressure Time **4 mins** Total Time **30 mins**

1 tsp avocado oil or olive oil

1 clove garlic, minced

6oz (170g) chickpea rotini

2 cups vegetable broth

¼ tsp red pepper flakes

½ tsp salt

1 cup finely chopped kale (stems removed and tightly packed)

⅓ cup half & half

2 tbsp shredded Parmesan cheese

For the sausage:
6oz (170g) ground pork

⅛ tsp garlic powder

⅛ tsp onion powder

½ tsp Italian seasoning

¼ tsp salt

¼ tsp black pepper

1. Prepare the sausage. In a small bowl, mix together the ground pork, garlic powder, onion powder, Italian seasoning, salt, and pepper. (This is easiest when done by hand.)

2. Select **Sauté (More)** and add the oil to the inner pot. When hot, add the sausage. Cook for 3 minutes, breaking up the sausage into large chunks. Add the minced garlic and sauté for 1 minute more. Press **Cancel.**

3. Add the rotini, vegetable broth, red pepper flakes, and salt, and stir to combine. Spread the kale over the pasta mixture.

4. Lock the lid and set the steam release valve to the sealing position. Select **Pressure Cook (High),** and set the cook time for **4 minutes.**

5. Once the cook time is complete, quick release the pressure. Stir in the half & half and Parmesan, and serve immediately.

TIP | Make it dairy-free: Substitute full-fat coconut milk for the half & half and omit or substitute the Parmesan with a vegan Parmesan alternative.

Take a shortcut by using 6 ounces (170g) premade Italian sausage instead of the from-scratch sausage mixture.

For a variation, try this recipe with chicken Italian sausage instead of pork.

NUTRITION PER SERVING:
Calories **580** • Total Fat **27.7g** • Total Carb **53g** • Fiber **9g** • Total Sugars **5g** • Protein **37g**

Garlic Butter Shrimp Scampi

This dish is low in carbs but still gets very high marks for taste and satisfaction. It features a rich buttery garlic sauce with delicately cooked, pink shrimp atop light, steamed spaghetti squash "noodles."

PROGRAM
Pressure Cook (High)

RELEASE
Quick

Gluten-Free, Keto Friendly

Serves **2**   Serving Size **about ¾ cup shrimp and sauce and ½ small spaghetti squash**   Prep Time **10 mins**   Pressure Time **8 mins**   Total Time **40 mins**

1 small spaghetti squash, about 1¼ lb (565g)

¼ cup Chicken Bone Broth (page 44) or store-bought chicken broth

2 round lemon slices, ¼ in (0.5cm) thick

2 tbsp salted butter

2 cloves garlic, sliced

Dash of red pepper flakes

½ tsp salt, plus more to taste

⅛ tsp black pepper, plus more to taste

10 frozen, peeled and deveined, tail-on, large or extra-large shrimp

1 tbsp finely chopped parsley

2 tbsp shaved Parmesan cheese

1. Rinse the outside of the spaghetti squash and slice in half lengthwise. Scoop out the seeds and discard.

2. Place the steam rack in the inner pot and add 1 cup water. Place the squash halves on the steam rack. Lock the lid and set the steam release valve to the sealing position. Select **Pressure Cook (High),** and set the cook time for **8 minutes.**

3. Once the cook time is complete, quick release the pressure. Carefully remove the squash halves from the inner pot and set aside. Remove the steam rack and discard the water.

4. Replace the inner pot and add the chicken broth, lemon slices, butter, garlic, red pepper flakes, salt, pepper, and frozen shrimp (make sure none of the shrimp are stuck together). Lock the lid and set the steam release valve to the sealing position. Select **Pressure Cook (High),** and set the cook time for **0 minutes.**

5. Season the squash halves with salt and pepper to taste. Fluff the spaghetti "noodles" with a fork and scoop out into a serving dish. Alternatively, leave the noodles in the skins, using them as bowls.

6. Once the cook time is complete, quick release the pressure. Stir in the parsley. Top the spaghetti squash with the shrimp and sauce, and sprinkle with Parmesan. Serve immediately.

TIP | Shrimp can overcook very quickly in the Instant Pot. To avoid ending up with rubbery scampi, this recipe starts with frozen shrimp.

NUTRITION PER SERVING:
Calories **323** • Total Fat **19.7g** • Total Carb **10g** • Fiber **3g** • Total Sugars **4g** • Protein **30g**

One-Pot Red Beans and Rice

From wholesome kidney beans to nourishing bone broth, this stick-to-your-ribs dinner comes packed with nutrients. It's hard to believe that this flavorful dish can be made in just one pot and in just 1 hour.

PROGRAM
**Sauté (More),
Pressure Cook (High)**

RELEASE
Natural and Quick

Gluten-Free, Dairy-Free Variation

Serves **2**　　Serving Size **about 2 cups**　　Prep Time **10 mins**　　Pressure Time **33 mins**　　Total Time **1 hour**

2 slices uncooked bacon, chopped

⅓ cup finely chopped yellow onion

⅓ cup finely chopped red bell pepper

1 medium stalk celery, finely chopped

1 clove garlic, minced

¼ tsp Creole seasoning

½ tsp dried thyme leaves

½ tsp salt

⅛ tsp black pepper

1 bay leaf

½ cup dried red kidney beans, rinsed

2 cups Chicken Bone Broth (page 44) or store-bought chicken broth

¾ cup white jasmine rice, rinsed

4oz (110g) smoked andouille sausage link, sliced in half lengthwise and chopped

2 tbsp sour cream, for serving

1 scallion, finely chopped, for serving

1. Select **Sauté (More).** When hot, add the bacon and sauté for 3 minutes, or until the fat begins to render. Add the onion, bell pepper, and celery, and sauté for 3 minutes more. Add the garlic, Creole seasoning, thyme, salt, pepper, and bay leaf. Sauté for 1 minute more.

2. Add the kidney beans and bone broth, and stir to combine. Lock the lid and set the steam release valve to the sealing position. Select **Pressure Cook (High),** and set the cook time for **25 minutes.**

3. Once the cook time is complete, allow the pressure to release naturally for 5 minutes, then quick release any remaining pressure. Press **Cancel** to turn off Keep Warm.

4. Stir the jasmine rice and chopped sausage into the inner pot. Lock the lid and set the steam release valve to the sealing position. Select **Pressure Cook (High),** and set the cook time for **8 minutes.**

5. Once the cook time is complete, allow the pressure to release naturally for 5 minutes, then quick release any remaining pressure. Remove and discard the bay leaf. Portion into 2 serving bowls and top each with sour cream and scallion. Serve immediately.

TIP | Make it dairy-free: Omit the sour cream.

Like it extra spicy? Increase the heat by doubling the Creole seasoning.

NUTRITION PER SERVING:
Calories **591** • Total Fat **20g** • Total Carb **69g** • Fiber **10g** • Total Sugars **6g** • Protein **30g**

One-Pot Chicken Teriyaki and Rice

There's no need to call for takeout when you can whip up this full teriyaki dinner in your Instant Pot at a moment's notice. Sweetness and umami combine beautifully to satisfy the craving with this one-pot meal.

PROGRAM
**Sauté (More),
Pressure Cook (High)**

RELEASE
Natural and Quick

**Gluten-Free,
Dairy-Free**

Serves **2**   Serving Size **about 1½ cups chicken and rice, and about ¾ cup cabbage**   Prep Time **10 mins**   Pressure Time **5 mins**   Total Time **40 mins**

1 tsp avocado oil or olive oil

10oz (285g) chicken thigh meat, diced

3 tbsp tamari

1 tbsp rice vinegar

¼ tsp ginger powder

¼ tsp garlic powder

¾ cup white jasmine rice, rinsed

¾ cup water

1 tbsp honey

1 tbsp coconut sugar

¼ medium green cabbage, sliced into 4 wedges

¼ tsp salt

½ tsp toasted sesame oil

Chopped scallions, for serving

Toasted sesame seeds, for serving

1. Select **Sauté (More),** and add the oil to the inner pot. When hot, add the chicken. Sauté for 5 minutes, or until the chicken is no longer pink. Press **Cancel.**

2. Add the tamari, rice vinegar, ginger, garlic powder, rice, and ¾ cup water to the inner pot, and stir to combine. Add the honey and coconut sugar, but do not stir.

3. Lay the cabbage wedges on top of the chicken and rice mixture. Do not stir. Lock the lid and set the steam release valve to the sealing position. Select **Pressure Cook (High),** and set the cook time for **5 minutes.**

4. Once the cook time is complete, allow the pressure to release naturally for 5 minutes, then quick release any remaining pressure. Remove the cabbage from the inner pot and season it with the salt and sesame oil.

5. Portion the chicken and rice into two serving bowls, and top each with scallions and a sprinkle of toasted sesame seeds. Serve immediately with the cabbage on the side.

TIP | Sugars like coconut sugar and honey tend to scorch on the bottom of the Instant Pot. To avoid this, they're added on top of the chicken and rice mixture but not stirred in until after cooking.

NUTRITION PER SERVING:
Calories **601** • Total Fat **13.9g** • Total Carb **82g** • Fiber **5g** • Total Sugars **19g** • Protein **36g**

Vegetarian Curried Lentil Stew

This is one of the dump-it-and-forget-it kinds of recipes for which the Instant Pot is known. The Instant Pot does all of the work to cook down these intense flavors and ingredients into a delicious and hearty stew.

PROGRAM
Pressure Cook (High), Sauté (More)

RELEASE
Natural and Quick

Gluten-Free, Dairy-Free, Vegan

Serves **2**   Serving Size **about 1¾ cups**   Prep Time **10 mins**   Pressure Time **15 mins**   Total Time **55 mins**

½ cup dried petite French green lentils, rinsed

2 cups vegetable broth

¼ cup finely chopped red onion

1 medium carrot, cut into ½in (1.25cm) pieces

½ medium red bell pepper, cut into ½in (1.25cm) squares

4oz (110g) peeled russet potato, cut into ½in (1.25cm) cubes (about 1 medium potato)

1 tbsp fresh lemon juice

1 tbsp tomato paste

2 tsp curry powder

¼ tsp ginger powder

¼ tsp garlic powder

¼ tsp smoked paprika

¾ tsp salt

¼ tsp black pepper

1 cup fresh baby spinach leaves (packed)

¼ cup full-fat coconut milk

Chopped cilantro, for garnish

Chopped red onion, for garnish

1. In the inner pot, stir together the lentils, vegetable broth, red onion, carrot, red bell pepper, potato, lemon juice, tomato paste, curry powder, ginger, garlic powder, paprika, salt, and pepper. Lock the lid and set the steam release valve to the sealing position. Select **Pressure Cook (High)**, and set the cook time for **15 minutes.**

2. Once the cook time is complete, allow the pressure to release naturally for 10 minutes, then quick release any remaining pressure. Press **Cancel** to turn off Keep Warm.

3. Select **Sauté (More)** and stir in the spinach and coconut milk. Bring just to a simmer to wilt the spinach, then remove the inner pot from the base. Portion the stew into two serving bowls and top with the cilantro and red onion. Serve immediately.

TIP | Pressure cooking breaks down foods so efficiently that meals can often end up with all of the ingredients being the same texture. Tricks used in this recipe, like stirring vegetables in at the last minute and garnishing with fresh, crunchy toppings, help diversify the texture palate.

NUTRITION PER SERVING:
Calories **336** • Total Fat **7.3g** • Total Carb **56g** • Fiber **11g** • Total Sugars **8g** • Protein **17g**

Minnesota Wild Rice Soup with Bacon

PROGRAM
Pressure Cook (High), Sauté (More)

RELEASE
Natural and Quick

Gluten-Free, Dairy-Free Variation

This simple and flavorful soup is sure to become a new favorite. It's perfectly thick and creamy. The nutty wild rice not only tastes delicious, but it is also an excellent source of dietary fiber.

Serves **2**   Serving Size **about 1¾ cups**   Prep Time **15 mins**   Pressure Time **30 mins**   Total Time **1 hour 25 mins**

¼ cup wild rice, rinsed

1 cup water

1 tsp salt, divided

4 slices uncooked bacon, chopped

½ cup diced yellow onion

½ cup diced celery (about 2 small stalks)

½ cup diced carrot (about 1 medium carrot)

1 cup chopped cremini mushrooms

¼ tsp garlic powder

½ tsp dried thyme leaves

⅛ tsp red pepper flakes

¼ tsp black pepper

1 cup Chicken Bone Broth (page 44) or store-bought chicken broth

4oz (110g) diced golden or red potatoes (peeled, if desired; about 1 medium potato)

1 tbsp arrowroot starch, or cornstarch

¼ cup half & half

Chopped parsley, for garnish

1. Combine the wild rice, 1 cup water, and ¼ teaspoon salt in the inner pot. Lock the lid and set the steam release valve to the sealing position. Select **Pressure Cook (High),** and set the cook time for **25 minutes.**

2. Once the cook time is complete, allow the pressure to release naturally for 10 minutes, then quick release any remaining pressure. Press **Cancel** to turn off Keep Warm. Using a mesh strainer, drain the wild rice and discard the excess liquid. Set aside.

3. Replace the inner pot and select **Sauté (More).** Add the bacon and cook until browned and crispy. Remove the bacon to a paper towel–lined plate and set aside.

4. Discard all but 1 tablespoon bacon fat from the inner pot. Add the onion, celery, and carrot, and sauté for 2 minutes. Add the mushrooms, garlic powder, thyme, red pepper flakes, ¾ teaspoon salt, and pepper, and sauté for 2 minutes more.

5. Add the broth, potato, and drained wild rice, and stir to combine. Lock the lid and set the steam release valve to the sealing position. Select **Pressure Cook (High),** and set the cook time for **5 minutes.**

6. Once the cook time is complete, allow the pressure to release naturally for 5 minutes, then quick release any remaining pressure. Press **Cancel** to turn off Keep Warm, and select **Sauté (More).** In a small bowl, mix together the starch and half & half, and stir into the inner pot. Bring just to a simmer, then remove the inner pot from the base. Stir in the bacon. Portion the soup into 2 serving bowls, and garnish each with a sprinkle of chopped parsley. Serve immediately.

Tip: Cooked wild rice freezes well. To cut down on prep at dinner time, cook a double batch of wild rice and freeze in two portions. At meal time, add in one of the frozen portions along with the broth and potatoes, and cook as directed (skipping steps 1–2).

Make it dairy-free: Substitute full-fat coconut milk for the half & half.

NUTRITION PER SERVING:
Calories **444** • Total Fat **24.9g** • Total Carb **38g** • Fiber **5g** • Total Sugars **7g** • Protein **19g**

Restaurant-Style Ramen Bowls

PROGRAM
**Sauté (More),
Pressure Cook (High)**

RELEASE
Quick

**Gluten-Free, Dairy-
Free, Keto-Friendly
Variation**

Now you can enjoy restaurant-quality ramen right at home and using only your Instant Pot. With so many irresistible flavors combined in one bowl, you'll be shocked that this recipe goes from start to finish in less than one hour.

Makes **2 ramen bowls**   Serving Size **1 ramen bowl**   Prep Time **25 mins**   Pressure Time **3 mins**   Total Time **40 mins**

2 tbsp avocado oil or olive oil, divided

1 small chicken breast, pounded to ½in (1.25cm) thick, seasoned with salt

1½ cups Chicken Bone Broth (page 44) or store-bought chicken broth

3 tbsp tamari

3 tbsp rice vinegar

1 tsp fish sauce

⅛ tsp red pepper flakes

2 scallions, white parts roughly chopped, and green parts chopped for garnish

½in (1.25cm) piece fresh ginger, sliced

1 clove garlic, sliced

2 squares uncooked Lotus Foods Millet & Brown Rice Ramen

Water, to cover

1 large egg

For serving:
2 tsp pickled ginger

2 tbsp thinly sliced nori

¼ cup thinly sliced purple cabbage

Toasted sesame seeds

2 lime wedges

1. Select **Sauté (More),** and heat 1 tablespoon oil in the inner pot. When hot, cook the chicken breast on one side for 6 minutes, then flip and cook for 4 minutes more, or until cooked through. Remove and set aside.

2. To the inner pot, add the broth, tamari, rice vinegar, fish sauce, red pepper flakes, white parts of the scallions, ginger, and garlic. Press **Cancel** to turn off Keep Warm.

3. Place the egg steamer trivet with 1½–2-inch (3.75–5cm) legs in the inner pot. In a 6-inch (15.25cm) round stainless steel pan, add the ramen squares, breaking them slightly so they lay in a single layer. Drizzle the noodles with the remaining 1 tablespoon oil, and add water just to cover.

4. Wash the outside of the egg and place it in the pan with the noodles. Cover the pan tightly with aluminum foil, and place on the steam rack. Lock the lid and set the steam release valve to the sealing position. Select **Pressure Cook (High),** and set the cook time for **3 minutes.** While the noodles are cooking, slice the chicken breast into strips and set aside. Prepare the garnishes for serving. Fill a small bowl with ice water.

5. Once the cook time is complete, quick release the pressure. Remove the egg from the pan and plunge immediately into the ice water. Drain the noodles using a fine-mesh strainer, and portion the noodles into two serving bowls. Using the fine-mesh strainer, strain the broth and discard the scallions, ginger, and garlic. Pour half of the broth over each serving.

6. Gently peel away the shell of the soft-boiled egg. Slice it in half, and place one half atop each bowl. Portion the sliced chicken breast into each bowl. Garnish with the green parts of the scallions, pickled ginger, nori, purple cabbage, sesame seeds, and a lime wedge. Serve immediately.

Tip: Make it keto friendly: Skip the ramen noodles and fill your bowl with uncooked spiralized zucchini noodles instead. Pour the hot broth over them, garnish with the toppings, and serve.

To make the dish easier to remove from the Instant Pot after cooking, make a sling for your pan with foil (page 13).

NUTRITION PER SERVING:
Calories **603** • Total Fat **22g** • Total Carb **54g** • Fiber **4g** • Total Sugars **3g** • Protein **49g**

One-Pot Pad Thai

Pad Thai might seem like an intimidating dish to attempt, but the Instant Pot makes it extremely easy and fast to throw together. The most challenging part of this recipe is just shopping for the ingredients!

PROGRAM
**Sauté (More),
Pressure Cook (Low)**

RELEASE
Natural and Quick

**Gluten-Free,
Dairy-Free**

Serves **2**   Serving Size **about 1¾ cups**   Prep Time **10 mins**   Pressure Time **1 min**   Total Time **30 mins**

1 tsp avocado oil or olive oil

4oz (110g) chicken thigh meat, cubed

4oz (110g) dry, flat stir-fry rice noodles

1 cup water

1 tbsp tamari

1 tsp fish sauce

1 tsp rice vinegar

1 tsp tamarind paste (optional)

¼ tsp garlic powder

¼ tsp red pepper flakes

4oz (110g) large uncooked shrimp, peeled, deveined, and tail-off

1 tbsp coconut sugar

2 scallions, white parts chopped into ½in (1.25cm) pieces, and green parts finely chopped for garnish

½ cup shredded carrot (about 1 medium carrot)

½ cup very thinly sliced red bell pepper (2in; 5cm strips; about ½ medium pepper)

½ cup fresh bean sprouts

2 tbsp chopped, roasted salted peanuts, for garnish

2 lime wedges, for garnish

1. Select **Sauté (More)** and add the oil to the inner pot. Once hot, add the chicken and sauté for 3 minutes, or until the meat is no longer pink. Press **Cancel.**

2. Break the noodles into about 6-inch (15.25cm) pieces and lay them in the inner pot over the chicken. Add 1 cup water, tamari, fish sauce, rice vinegar, tamarind paste (if using), garlic powder, and red pepper flakes. Lock the lid and set the steam release valve to the sealing position. Select **Pressure Cook (Low)** and set the cook time for **1 minute.**

3. Once the cook time is complete, allow the pressure to release naturally for 5 minutes, then quick release any remaining pressure.

4. Stir in the shrimp, coconut sugar, white parts of the scallions, carrot, bell pepper, and bean sprouts. Lock the lid again and allow the pot to sit on **Keep Warm** for 5 minutes. (The pot will switch to the **Keep Warm** setting automatically after pressure cooking, so there is no need to select the button.) This small amount of heat will be enough to cook the shrimp.

5. Open the lid and stir. Make sure the shrimp are pink and cooked through. If not fully pink, replace the lid and let sit for another 1 to 2 minutes.

6. Portion the pad Thai into 2 serving bowls, and garnish each with a sprinkle of the green parts of the scallions, chopped peanuts, and a lime wedge. Serve immediately.

TIP | Tamarind paste adds a unique and delicious flavor to this pad Thai, but it can be omitted.

Simplify this recipe by using double the chicken and omitting the shrimp.

Sugars have a tendency to scorch on the bottom of the Instant Pot. To avoid this, the coconut sugar isn't stirred in till the very end.

Shrimp can overcook very quickly under pressure. The residual heat from the pot is plenty to cook the shrimp while still keeping them succulent and tender.

NUTRITION PER SERVING (EXCLUDING TAMARIND PASTE):
Calories **486** • Total Fat **12.7g** • Total Carb **60g** • Fiber **4g** • Total Sugars **8g** • Protein **33g**

Thai Peanut Pork Curry

This high-protein dish is deliciously creamy and bursting with so many flavors. The pork is pressure cooked with the peanut sauce to a tender perfection and then complemented by crisp veggies and crunchy roasted peanuts.

PROGRAM
**Sauté (More),
Pressure Cook (High)**

RELEASE
Natural and Quick

**Gluten-Free,
Dairy-Free**

Serves **2**   Serving Size **about 1 cup**   Prep Time **20 mins**   Pressure Time **8 mins**   Total Time **45 mins**

1 tsp avocado oil or olive oil

10oz (285g) boneless pork shoulder, trimmed of fat and cut into thin strips

2 tbsp water

1 batch Pot-in-Pot White Rice (optional; see page 94)

¼ cup sliced red onion (2in; 5cm long)

½ cup sliced yellow bell pepper (2in; 5cm strips)

½ cup julienned carrots

¼ cup fresh basil leaves (packed)

1 tbsp chopped, roasted, and salted peanuts

½ cup fresh bean sprouts

2 lime wedges

For the Thai Peanut Sauce:
3 tbsp creamy peanut butter

2 tsp coconut sugar

1 tbsp tamari

½ tsp toasted sesame oil

1 tbsp rice vinegar

1 tbsp lime juice

1 tsp red curry paste

⅛ tsp red pepper flakes

⅛ tsp ginger powder

⅛ tsp garlic powder

1 tbsp full-fat coconut milk

1. Prepare the Thai Peanut Sauce. In a small bowl, whisk together the peanut butter, coconut sugar, tamari, sesame oil, rice vinegar, lime juice, red curry paste, red pepper flakes, ginger, garlic powder, and coconut milk.

2. Select **Sauté (More)** and add the oil to the inner pot. When hot, add the pork and sauté for 6 minutes. Press **Cancel** to turn off Sauté. Add 2 tablespoons water to the inner pot, and pour the peanut sauce over the meat, but do not stir.

3. If cooking Pot-in-Pot White rice, add the egg steamer trivet with 1½–2-inch (3.75–5cm) legs to the inner pot. Place the pan of white rice, water, and salt on the trivet above the pork mixture. (See page 94 for the complete recipe.) Lock the lid and set the steam release valve to the sealing position. Select **Pressure Cook (High),** and set the cook time for **8 minutes.**

4. Once the cook time is complete, allow the pressure to release naturally for 5 minutes, then quick release any remaining pressure. Press **Cancel** to turn off Keep Warm. Remove the rice pan and egg steamer trivet from the inner pot (if applicable).

5. Select **Sauté (More),** and add the onion, bell pepper, and carrots. Stir and simmer for 3 minutes, or until the vegetables begin to soften. Remove the inner pot from the base, and stir in the basil.

6. Portion out the rice (if using) and curry into two serving bowls. Top each serving with a sprinkle of chopped peanuts, bean sprouts, and a lime wedge. Serve immediately.

TIP | You can substitute chopped chicken breast or chicken thigh meat for the pork shoulder.

NUTRITION PER SERVING (EXCLUDING RICE):
Calories **493** • Total Fat **31.2g** • Total Carb **19g** • Fiber **4g** • Total Sugars **8g** • Protein **37g**

Massaman Chicken Curry

Intense flavors are the hallmark of this creamy yet dairy-free curry dish. Waiting until the end of cooking to add the vegetables leaves them with a nice crunch while still allowing the chicken to become fall-apart tender.

PROGRAM
**Sauté (More),
Pressure Cook (High),
Sauté (Normal)**

RELEASE
Natural and Quick

**Gluten-Free,
Dairy-Free**

Serves **2**　　Serving Size **about 1½ cups**　　Prep Time **5 mins**　　Pressure Time **6 mins**　　Total Time **35 mins**

1 tbsp avocado oil or olive oil

12oz (340g) boneless, skinless chicken thighs, diced

¼ cup Chicken Bone Broth (page 44) or store-bought chicken broth

1 cup diced red or Yukon Gold potatoes

1 tsp salt

1 clove garlic, minced

1 tsp minced fresh ginger

2 tsp massaman curry paste (see tip)

½ cup chopped red bell pepper (1in; 2.5cm pieces)

½ cup chopped snow peas (1in; 2.5cm pieces)

½ cup chopped baby corn spears (1in; 2.5cm pieces)

¼ cup chopped red onion (1in; 2.5cm pieces)

½ cup full-fat coconut milk

1 tbsp chopped cilantro, for garnish

2 lime wedges, for garnish

1. Select **Sauté (More)** and add the oil to the inner pot. When hot, add the chicken. Sauté for 6 minutes, or until the chicken is no longer pink.

2. Add the broth, potatoes, salt, garlic, ginger, and curry paste. Press **Cancel** to turn off Keep Warm. Lock the lid and set the steam release valve to the sealing position. Select **Pressure Cook (High),** and set the cook time for **6 minutes.**

3. Once the cook time is complete, allow the pressure to release naturally for 5 minutes, then quick release any remaining pressure. Press **Cancel** to turn off Keep Warm.

4. Select **Sauté (Normal),** and add the red bell pepper, snow peas, baby corn, red onion, and coconut milk. Stir to combine and allow to simmer for 4 minutes, or until the vegetables just begin to soften.

5. Portion into two serving bowls and top with a sprinkle of cilantro and a lime wedge. Serve immediately.

TIP　Make this a one-pot meal by cooking white rice at the same time as the curry using the "pot-in-pot" cooking method (page 94).

Massaman curry paste can often be found at health food stores in the international or Asian foods section. If you can't find massaman curry paste locally, you can order online or substitute with red curry paste.

Baby corn spears are often found canned in the international or Asian foods section. If you have difficulty finding some, substitute the fresh crunch with either ¼ cup canned sliced water chestnuts (drained) or ¼ cup canned bamboo shoots (drained).

NUTRITION PER SERVING:
Calories **434** • Total Fat **19.6g** • Total Carb **26g** • Fiber **4g** • Total Sugars **5g** • Protein **39g**

Beef Stew with Parsnips

Parsnips tend to be an underrated vegetable, but they have such a unique and delicious flavor. In this stew, the natural sweetness from the parsnips and balsamic vinegar balances out nicely with rich beef broth and the kick of black pepper.

PROGRAM
**Sauté (More),
Pressure Cook (High)**

RELEASE
Natural and Quick

**Gluten-Free,
Dairy-Free, Keto-
Friendly Variation**

Serves **2**   Serving Size **about 1¾ cups**   Prep Time **20 mins**   Pressure Time **10 mins**   Total Time **1 hour 30 mins**

1 tsp salt

½ tsp black pepper

4 tsp arrowroot starch, or cornstarch

8oz (225g) beef stew meat, cut into 1in (2.5cm) cubes

1 tbsp avocado oil or olive oil

½ cup diced yellow onion

1 cup beef broth

2 medium parsnips, cut into 1in (2.5cm) pieces

2 medium carrots, cut into 1in (2.5cm) chunks

1 bay leaf

¾ tsp dried thyme leaves (or 2 tsp fresh thyme leaves)

½ tsp garlic powder

1 tbsp balsamic vinegar

1 tbsp chopped parsley

1. In a medium bowl, combine the salt, pepper, and starch. Toss the meat in the starch mixture until evenly coated.

2. Select **Sauté (More),** and add the oil to the inner pot. When hot, add the onion and sauté for 2 minutes. Add the meat mixture and sauté for 5 minutes more or until the meat is browned.

3. Pour in the beef broth and scrape the bottom of the inner pot to lift any browned bits stuck to the bottom. Add the parsnips, carrots, bay leaf, thyme, garlic powder, and balsamic vinegar, and stir to combine. Press **Cancel** to turn off Sauté.

4. Lock the lid and set the steam release valve to the sealing position. Select **Pressure Cook (High),** and set the cook time for **10 minutes.**

5. Once the cook time is complete, allow the pressure to release naturally for 5 minutes, then quick release any remaining pressure.

6. Discard the bay leaf. Stir in the chopped parsley, and serve immediately.

| TIP | Make it keto friendly: You can drastically cut down carbs by replacing the parsnips with red or daikon radishes. |

NUTRITION PER SERVING:

Calories **381** • Total Fat **12.4g** • Total Carb **41g** • Fiber **9g** • Total Sugars **12g** • Protein **29g**

Classic Beef Stroganoff

This stroganoff is deliciously creamy and full of flavor while being naturally low in carbs. It pairs beautifully with rice or noodles, but you can keep the meal low-carb by serving with cauliflower rice or spaghetti squash.

PROGRAM
**Sauté (More),
Pressure Cook (High)**

RELEASE
Natural and Quick

**Gluten-Free,
Dairy-Free Variation,
Keto Friendly**

Serves **2**   Serving Size **about ¾ cup**   Prep Time **15 mins**   Pressure Time **8 mins**   Total Time **40 mins**

1 tsp avocado oil or olive oil

8oz (225g) sirloin steak, cut into thin strips

½ cup diced yellow onion

3oz (85g) sliced fresh mushrooms (about 1 cup)

¼ cup beef broth or water

1 tsp red wine vinegar

1 tsp Worcestershire sauce

¼ tsp garlic powder

½ tsp salt

½ tsp black pepper

1 tsp arrowroot starch, or cornstarch

1 tbsp water

3 tbsp sour cream

1 tbsp chopped parsley

1. Select **Sauté (More),** and add the oil to the inner pot. When hot, add the steak. Sauté for 4 minutes or until the steak is no longer pink.

2. Add the onion and mushrooms, and sauté for 2 minutes more. Stir in the broth, red wine vinegar, Worcestershire sauce, garlic powder, salt, and pepper. Press **Cancel** to turn off Sauté.

3. Lock the lid and set the steam release valve to the sealing position. Select **Pressure Cook (High),** and set the cook time for **8 minutes.** In a small bowl, mix together the starch and 1 tablespoon water, and set aside.

4. Once the cook time is complete, allow the pressure to release naturally for 5 minutes, then quick release any remaining pressure.

5. Press **Cancel** to turn off Keep Warm, and select **Sauté (More).** Stir in the starch mixture and sour cream. Bring just to a simmer, then remove the inner pot from the base. Stir in the parsley and serve immediately.

TIP | Make it dairy-free: Substitute 3 tablespoons full-fat coconut milk for the sour cream.

This recipe is very low in carbs, but you can reduce them even further by omitting the arrowroot or cornstarch thickener.

For easy slicing, place the steak into the freezer for about 10 minutes before cutting into strips.

NUTRITION PER SERVING (USING BEEF BROTH):
Calories **308** • Total Fat **19.2g** • Total Carb **8g** • Fiber **1g** • Total Sugars **3g** • Protein **25g**

Creamy Corn Chowder

This recipe could have easily been named Rainbow Chowder. It has red peppers, orange carrots, yellow corn, green chives, and purple onions. Serve in a blue bowl and you will account for all of the colors of the rainbow!

PROGRAM
Pressure Cook (High), Sauté (More)

RELEASE
Natural and Quick

Gluten-Free, Dairy-Free Variation, Vegan Variation

Serves **2**   Serving Size **about 1¾ cups**   Prep Time **10 mins**   Pressure Time **4 mins**   Total Time **30 mins**

1 cup vegetable broth

1 cup yellow sweet corn kernels (fresh, frozen, or canned and drained)

8oz (225g) peeled and diced russet potatoes (about 2 small potatoes)

¼ cup diced red onion

½ cup diced carrot (about 1 medium carrot)

½ cup diced celery (about 2 small stalks)

½ cup diced red bell pepper (about ½ medium pepper)

¼ tsp garlic powder

¼ tsp smoked paprika

¼ tsp dried thyme leaves

1 bay leaf

¾ tsp salt

¼ tsp black pepper

¼ cup heavy whipping cream

1 tbsp arrowroot starch, or cornstarch

Finely chopped chives, for garnish

1. In the inner pot, stir together the vegetable broth, corn kernels, potatoes, red onion, carrot, celery, red pepper, garlic powder, paprika, thyme, bay leaf, salt, and pepper.

2. Lock the lid and set the steam release valve to the sealing position. Select **Pressure Cook (High),** and set the cook time for **4 minutes.** In a small bowl, mix together the cream and the starch. Set aside.

3. Once the cook time is complete, allow the pressure to release naturally for 5 minutes, then quick release any remaining pressure. Press **Cancel** to turn off Keep Warm.

4. Select **Sauté (More),** and stir in the cream and starch mixture. Bring just to a simmer to thicken, then remove the inner pot from the base. Portion into two serving bowls, and top with a sprinkle of chives. Serve immediately.

TIP | Make it dairy-free and vegan: Substitute full-fat coconut milk for the heavy whipping cream.

NUTRITION PER SERVING:
Calories **313** • Total Fat **12.2g** • Total Carb **49g** • Fiber **6g** • Total Sugars **11g** • Protein **7g**

No-Dairy New England Clam Chowder

PROGRAM
**Sauté (More),
Pressure Cook (High)**

RELEASE
Natural and Quick

**Gluten-Free,
Dairy-Free**

Using coconut milk is an excellent way to enjoy thick and creamy soups and chowders while avoiding dairy. Tender potatoes, smoky bacon, and chewy clams all come together for this deliciously creamy and satisfying chowder.

Serves **2**   Serving Size **about 1¾ cups**   Prep Time **15 mins**   Pressure Time **3 mins**   Total Time **40 mins**

2 slices uncooked bacon, chopped

¼ cup diced yellow onion

½ cup diced celery (about 2 small stalks)

½ cup diced carrots (about 1 medium carrot)

1 clove garlic, minced

½ tsp ground thyme

¼ tsp smoked paprika

½ tsp salt

¼ tsp black pepper

¾ cup vegetable broth

8oz (225g) peeled and diced russet potatoes (about 2 small potatoes)

1 bay leaf

1 (6.5oz; 185g) can chopped or minced clams, liquid reserved

½ cup full-fat coconut milk

1 tbsp arrowroot starch, or cornstarch

1 tbsp chopped parsley

1. Select **Sauté (More).** Add the bacon to the inner pot and cook until browned and crispy. Remove the bacon to a paper towel–lined plate, leaving the rendered bacon fat in the pot.

2. Add the onion, celery, and carrot to the inner pot and sauté for 3 minutes. Add the garlic, thyme, paprika, salt, and pepper, and sauté for 1 minute more.

3. Press **Cancel** to turn off Sauté. Stir in the vegetable broth, potatoes, bay leaf, and the liquid from the can of clams.

4. Lock the lid and set the steam release valve to the sealing position. Select **Pressure Cook (High),** and set the cook time for **3 minutes.** In a small bowl, mix together the coconut milk and starch.

5. Once the cook time is complete, allow the pressure to release naturally for 5 minutes, then quick release any remaining pressure. Press **Cancel** to turn off Keep Warm, and select **Sauté (More).**

6. Stir in the clams and the coconut milk and starch mixture. Bring just to a simmer, then remove the inner pot from the base. Discard the bay leaf, and stir in the parsley and bacon crumbles. Serve immediately.

TIP Cooking clams under pressure for any amount of time would result in a rubberlike texture. To avoid this, they're added in after the pressure cooking time is complete and simmered just long enough to heat them up.

NUTRITION PER SERVING:
Calories **363** • Total Fat **22.9g** • Total Carb **34g** • Fiber **4g** • Total Sugars **4g** • Protein **9g**

Autumn Pumpkin Chili

While it may taste like it's been simmering for hours, this dish cooks to perfection in just 35 minutes under pressure. These piping hot bowls of nourishing chili are an ideal way to warm you inside and out on a dreary day.

PROGRAM
**Sauté (More),
Pressure Cook (High)**

RELEASE
Natural and Quick

**Gluten-Free,
Dairy-Free**

Serves **2**　　　Serving Size **1½ cups**　　　Prep Time **25 mins**　　　Pressure Time **35 mins**　　　Total Time **1 hour 25 mins**

1 tsp avocado oil or olive oil

6oz (170g) 90% lean ground beef

½ cup chopped yellow onion

2oz (55g) canned diced green chiles

1½ tsp chili powder

½ tsp ground cumin

½ tsp dried oregano

½ tsp ground cinnamon

¼ tsp garlic powder

¼ tsp smoked paprika

¼ tsp black pepper

1 tsp salt

1¼ cups Chicken Bone Broth (page 44) or store-bought chicken broth

¼ cup dried black beans, rinsed

¼ cup dried red kidney beans, rinsed

½ cup diced fresh tomatoes (about ½ medium tomato), or canned petite-diced tomatoes

½ cup pumpkin purée, canned or fresh

For serving:
½ medium avocado, chopped

Chopped cilantro

Chopped red onion

1. Select **Sauté (More),** and add the oil to the inner pot. When hot, add the ground beef, onion, and green chiles. Sauté for 6 minutes, breaking up the beef into little pieces until it is no longer pink.

2. Mix in the chili powder, cumin, oregano, cinnamon, garlic powder, paprika, pepper, and salt, and sauté for 1 minute more. Press **Cancel** to turn off Sauté.

3. Add the bone broth, black beans, and kidney beans, and stir to combine. Make sure all of the beans are fully submerged in the liquid. Add the diced tomato and pumpkin purée on top, and do not stir.

4. Lock the lid and set the steam release valve to the sealing position. Select **Pressure Cook (High),** and set the cook time for **35 minutes.**

5. Once the cook time is complete, allow the pressure to release naturally for 15 minutes, then quick release any remaining pressure. Portion the chili into two serving bowls and top with avocado, cilantro, and red onion. Serve immediately.

TIP　Thick ingredients like tomatoes and purées are known to scorch on the bottom of the Instant Pot and give a Burn error message. This recipe avoids that possibility by adding the tomato and pumpkin purée at the very end and not stirring it into the rest of the ingredients until the cook time is finished.

This chili pairs beautifully with the Cornbread Bundtlet on page 117.

NUTRITION PER SERVING:
Calories **479** • Total Fat **15.2g** • Total Carb **44g** • Fiber **13g** • Total Sugars **6g** • Protein **40g**

White Chicken Chili

This chili is rich and velvety with just the right amount of spice. It's so easy to throw into the pot and then let the Instant Pot work its magic to transform all of the ingredients into piping hot bowls of nourishment.

PROGRAM
Pressure Cook (High)

RELEASE
Natural and Quick

Gluten-Free, Dairy-Free Variation

Serves **2**   Serving Size **about 1¾ cups**   Prep Time **5 mins**   Pressure Time **35 mins**   Total Time **1 hour 20 mins**

1½ cups Chicken Bone Broth (page 44) or store-bought chicken broth

½ cup dried navy beans, rinsed

½ cup diced yellow onion

1 (4oz; 110g) can fire-roasted diced green chilies

½ tsp dried oregano

¼ tsp garlic powder

¼ tsp chili powder

¼ tsp cumin powder

1 tsp salt

¼ tsp black pepper

8oz (225g) chicken breast (1 breast)

2oz (55g) ⅓-less-fat cream cheese

For serving:
½ cup chopped avocado

Chopped cilantro

Minced red onion

1. To the inner pot, add the broth, beans, onion, green chilies, oregano, garlic powder, chili powder, cumin, salt, and pepper. Stir to combine. Make sure all of the beans are covered with liquid, and place the chicken breast on top of the mixture.

2. Lock the lid and set the steam release valve to the sealing position. Select **Pressure Cook (High),** and set the cook time for **35 minutes.**

3. Once the cook time is complete, allow the pressure to release naturally for 15 minutes, then quick release any remaining pressure. Remove the chicken breast from the pot, shred, and finely chop.

4. Using a potato masher, mash the beans in the inner pot 5 to 6 times to thicken the broth slightly. Add the chopped chicken breast back to the inner pot along with the cream cheese. Stir until the cream cheese is melted and fully incorporated.

5. Portion the chili into 2 serving bowls, and top each with ¼ cup chopped avocado and a sprinkle of cilantro and red onion. Serve immediately.

TIP | Make it dairy-free: Substitute ¼ cup full-fat coconut milk for the cream cheese.

NUTRITION PER SERVING:

Calories **500** • Total Fat **14.6g** • Total Carb **46g** • Fiber **13g** • Total Sugars **8g** • Protein **49g**

Red Lentil Chicken Stew with Quinoa

PROGRAM
**Sauté (More),
Pressure Cook (High)**

RELEASE
Natural and Quick

**Gluten-Free,
Dairy-Free**

This savory high-protein stew is very simple but oh so satisfying. The quinoa provides delicious texture, and the red lentils cook down into the broth to thicken and add amazing flavor.

Serves **2**   Serving Size **about 2 cups**   Prep Time **15 mins**   Pressure Time **3 mins**   Total Time **35 mins**

1 tsp avocado oil or olive oil

8oz (225g) chicken thigh meat (excess fat trimmed), cubed

½ cup diced yellow onion (about ½ small onion)

½ cup diced red bell pepper (about ½ medium pepper)

½ cup diced celery (about 2 small stalks)

2 tsp fresh thyme leaves, or ½ tsp dried thyme leaves

1 clove garlic, minced

1 tsp salt

¼ tsp black pepper

2 cups Chicken Bone Broth (page 44) or store-bought chicken broth

¼ cup dried split red lentils, rinsed

¼ cup quinoa

Chopped parsley, for garnish

1. Select **Sauté (More),** and add the oil to the inner pot. When hot, add the chicken and sauté for 4 minutes, or until it is no longer pink.

2. Add the onion, red bell pepper, celery, thyme, garlic, salt, and pepper. Sauté for 3 minutes more.

3. Press **Cancel** and stir in the broth, red lentils, and quinoa.

4. Lock the lid and set the steam release valve to the sealing position. Select **Pressure Cook (High),** and set the cook time for **3 minutes.**

5. Once the cook time is complete, allow the pressure to release naturally for 5 minutes, then quick release any remaining pressure.

6. Portion the stew into two serving bowls and garnish each with chopped parsley. Serve immediately.

TIP | Check your package of quinoa to see if it is prewashed. If it is not, rinse it well with a fine-mesh strainer before cooking to remove the bitter, naturally occurring saponins.

NUTRITION PER SERVING:
Calories **436** • Total Fat **13.4g** • Total Carb **37g** • Fiber **11g** • Total Sugars **5g** • Protein **41g**

Caribbean-Inspired Pork and Plantain Stew

PROGRAM
**Sauté (More),
Pressure Cook (High)**

RELEASE
Natural and Quick

**Gluten-Free,
Dairy-Free**

This sweet and savory dish delivers on many levels. A thick and meaty stew as the base is then topped with a deliciously fresh and vibrantly colored mango and avocado salsa. It's immensely satisfying and refreshing!

Serves **2** Serving Size **about 1½ cups stew and ½ cup salsa** Prep Time **15 mins** Pressure Time **8 mins** Total Time **40 mins**

6oz (170g) boneless pork shoulder

1 small, ripe plantain

1 tbsp avocado oil or olive oil

¼ cup chopped red onion

½ cup No-Fuss Black Beans (page 109) or canned black beans, drained

1 cup Chicken Bone Broth (page 44) or store-bought chicken broth

⅛ tsp chipotle powder

¼ tsp ginger powder

⅛ tsp allspice

⅛ tsp garlic powder

¼ tsp salt

⅛ tsp black pepper

For the mango-avocado salsa:

½ mango, peeled and chopped

½ medium avocado, chopped

½ medium jalapeño, deseeded and minced

2 tbsp minced red onion

Juice of ½ lime

1 tbsp finely chopped cilantro

⅛ tsp salt

⅛ tsp black pepper

1. Trim the fat from the pork shoulder. Cut into ½-inch (1.25cm) cubes. Quarter the plantain lengthwise, and chop into ½-inch (1.25cm) pieces.

2. Select **Sauté (More),** and heat the oil in the inner pot. When hot, add the pork, onion, and plantain. Sauté for 5 minutes, or until the meat is no longer pink and the onions and plantain begin to soften. Press **Cancel** to turn off Sauté.

3. Add the black beans, bone broth, chipotle powder, ginger, allspice, garlic powder, salt, and pepper, and stir to combine. Lock the lid and set the steam release valve to the sealing position. Select **Pressure Cook (High),** and set the cook time for **8 minutes.**

4. Meanwhile, make the mango-avocado salsa. In a small bowl, combine the mango, avocado, jalapeño, onion, lime juice, cilantro, salt, and pepper. Gently toss until thoroughly mixed. Cover and chill in the refrigerator until the stew is ready to serve.

5. Once the cook time is complete, allow the pressure to release naturally for 5 minutes, then quick release any remaining pressure. Portion the stew into two serving bowls, and top each with a scoop of mango-avocado salsa. Serve immediately.

TIP | Do yourself a favor and make a double batch of the mango-avocado salsa! One taste and you'll find yourself wanting to put it on everything or just eat it by the spoonful.

NUTRITION PER SERVING:
Calories **541** • Total Fat **16.8g** • Total Carb **75g** • Fiber **11g** • Total Sugars **37g** • Protein **31g**

Nourishing Chicken Noodle Soup

The spices, herbs, and savory chicken bone broth are the perfect prescription for coaxing anyone who is under the weather back to health. This wholesome soup truly nourishes the body and the soul.

PROGRAM
**Sauté (More),
Pressure Cook (High)**

RELEASE
Natural and Quick

**Gluten-Free Variation,
Dairy-Free**

Serves **2**   Serving Size **1¾ cups**   Prep Time **15 mins**   Pressure Time **1 min**   Total Time **35 mins**

1 tsp avocado oil or olive oil

¼ cup diced yellow onion

½ cup diced celery (about 2 small stalks)

1 cup diced carrot (about 2 medium carrots)

1 clove garlic, minced

2 tsp chopped fresh thyme leaves (or ½ tsp dried thyme leaves)

2 tsp chopped fresh rosemary (or ½ tsp dried rosemary)

½ tsp salt

¼ tsp black pepper

2½ cups Chicken Bone Broth (page 44) or store-bought chicken broth

1 cup shredded, cooked chicken breast

1 cup uncooked wide egg noodles

2 tbsp chopped parsley

1. Select **Sauté (More),** and add the oil to the inner pot. When hot, add the onion, celery, and carrot, and sauté for 3 minutes. Add the garlic, thyme, rosemary, salt, and pepper, and sauté for 1 minute more.

2. Press **Cancel** to turn off Sauté, and stir in the broth, shredded chicken, and noodles. Lock the lid and set the steam release valve to the sealing position. Select **Pressure Cook (High),** and set the cook time for **1 minute.**

3. Once the cook time is complete, allow the pressure to release naturally for 5 minutes, then quick release any remaining pressure. Stir in the parsley and serve immediately.

TIP | Make it gluten-free: Because gluten-free pasta tends to release a lot of starch while cooking, prepare your favorite noodles on the stove according to the package directions and drain. Stir the cooked pasta into the soup after the pressure cooking time has finished, along with the parsley.

NUTRITION PER SERVING:

Calories **277** • Total Fat **6.3g** • Total Carb **24g** • Fiber **4g** • Total Sugars **5g** • Protein **31g**

Egg Drop Soup

This soup cooks up so quickly that you won't even have to use a pressure setting on your Instant Pot. It's flavorful, satisfying, and simple—a wonderful appetizer or a deliciously light dinner.

PROGRAM
Sauté (More)

RELEASE
None

Gluten-Free, Dairy-Free, Keto Friendly

Serves **2**   Serving Size **about 1½ cups**   Prep Time **5 mins**   Pressure Time **None**   Total Time **15 mins**

2½ cups Chicken Bone Broth (page 44) or store-bought chicken broth

¼ tsp ginger powder

¼ tsp garlic powder

⅛ tsp black pepper

1 tbsp tamari

1 tbsp arrowroot starch, or cornstarch

1 large egg, well beaten

1 scallion, finely chopped

1. Select **Sauté (More),** and add the broth, ginger, garlic powder, and pepper to the inner pot. Bring to a simmer.

2. In a small bowl, mix together the tamari and starch. Stir the mixture into the inner pot.

3. Once the broth has begun to simmer again, stir in a circular motion with a nonslotted spoon. While continuing to stir, pour the beaten egg into the broth in a thin stream. The egg will cook on contact with the hot broth.

4. Stir in the chopped scallion, and serve immediately.

TIP | This soup is already very low carb, but you can omit the arrowroot or cornstarch thickener to cut down carbs even more.

NUTRITION PER SERVING:
Calories **65** • Total Fat **2.4g** • Total Carb **5g** • Fiber **1g** • Total Sugars **1g** • Protein **6g**

Green Chile Pork and Potato Stew

This frugal dinner comes together so quickly in the Instant Pot. The green chilies add delicious flavor without adding too much heat, and the bit of creaminess at the end from the half & half brings together this smooth and hearty stew.

PROGRAM
**Sauté (More),
Pressure Cook (High)**

RELEASE
Natural and Quick

Gluten-Free, Dairy-Free Variation

Serves **2** · Serving Size **about 1¾ cups** · Prep Time **15 mins** · Pressure Time **6 mins** · Total Time **40 mins**

1 tsp avocado oil or olive oil

¼ cup diced red onion

½ cup diced carrot (about 1 medium carrot)

8oz (225g) boneless pork shoulder, trimmed of fat and cut into ½in (1.25cm) cubes

1 (4oz; 110g) can fire-roasted diced green chilies

¼ tsp garlic powder

½ tsp chili powder

½ tsp dried oregano

1 tsp salt

¼ tsp black pepper

1 cup vegetable broth

8oz (225g) golden or red potatoes, cut into ½in (1.25cm) cubes (about 2 medium potatoes; optional to peel)

¼ cup half & half

Minced red onion, for garnish

Chopped cilantro, for garnish

1. Select **Sauté (More),** and add the oil to the inner pot. When hot, add the onion and carrot, and sauté for 2 minutes.

2. Add the pork and sauté for 5 minutes more. Stir in the green chilies, garlic powder, chili powder, oregano, salt, and pepper, and sauté for 1 minute more.

3. Press **Cancel** to turn off Sauté. Stir in the broth and potatoes. Lock the lid and set the steam release valve to the sealing position. Select **Pressure Cook (High),** and set the cook time for **6 minutes.**

4. Once the cook time is complete, allow the pressure to release naturally for 5 minutes, then quick release any remaining pressure. Press **Cancel** to turn off Keep Warm, and select **Sauté (More).** Stir in the half & half. Bring just up to a simmer, then remove the inner pot from the base.

5. Portion the stew into two serving bowls and garnish each with a sprinkle of red onion and cilantro. Serve immediately.

TIP | Try this dish with cubed chicken breast or chicken thigh meat instead of pork.

Make it dairy-free: Substitute full-fat coconut milk for the half & half.

NUTRITION PER SERVING:
Calories **341** • Total Fat **12.7g** • Total Carb **32g** • Fiber **5g** • Total Sugars **8g** • Protein **26g**

Cheesy Broccoli and Rice Soup

This soup is a perfect comfort food for cool fall days. Broccoli and Cheddar are obviously a match made in heaven. When rounded out with rice and a rich broth, satisfaction is taken to the next level.

PROGRAM
**Sauté (Normal),
Pressure Cook (High),
Sauté (Less)**

RELEASE
Natural and Quick

Gluten-Free, Dairy-Free Variation, Vegan Variation

Serves **2**   Serving Size **about 1½ cups**   Prep Time **15 mins**   Pressure Time **2 mins**   Total Time **40 mins**

1 tsp avocado oil or olive oil

¼ cup diced yellow onion

½ cup diced celery (about 2 small stalks)

½ cup diced carrot (about 1 medium carrot)

1 clove garlic, minced

2 cups vegetable broth

¾ tsp salt

¼ tsp black pepper

¼ cup white jasmine or long-grain white rice, rinsed

4oz (110g) fresh or frozen broccoli florets (about 2 cups)

¼ cup half & half

¼ cup shredded Cheddar cheese

1. Select **Sauté (Normal)** and add the oil to the inner pot. When hot, add the onion, celery, and carrot. Sauté for 3 minutes. Add the garlic and sauté for 1 minute more.

2. Press **Cancel** to turn off Sauté. Stir in the vegetable broth, salt, pepper, and rice. Lock the lid and set the steam release valve to the sealing position. Select **Pressure Cook (High),** and set the cook time for **2 minutes.**

3. Once the cook time is complete, allow the pressure to release naturally for 5 minutes, then quick release any remaining pressure.

4. Press **Cancel** to turn off Keep Warm, and select **Sauté (Less).** Stir in the broccoli florets and allow them to simmer for 5 minutes, or until they reach the desired tenderness. Stir the soup constantly to help keep the rice from sticking to the bottom of the inner pot.

5. Add the half & half and Cheddar, and stir until the cheese is melted and smooth. Remove from the heat and serve immediately.

TIP | Make it dairy-free and vegan: Substitute full-fat coconut milk for the half & half and use 2 tablespoons nutritional yeast flakes in place of the shredded Cheddar.

NUTRITION PER SERVING:
Calories **272** • Total Fat **11.7g** • Total Carb **33g** • Fiber **4g** • Total Sugars **6g** • Protein **10g**

Jalapeño Popper Soup with Sausage

PROGRAM
**Sauté (More),
Pressure Cook (High)**

RELEASE
Natural and Quick

**Gluten-Free,
Keto Friendly**

From home-mixed sausage to shredded Cheddar and cream cheese, the classic jalapeño popper flavor dominates this warm and comforting dish. This rich soup is surprisingly low in carbs but still full of flavor and spice.

Serves **2**   Serving Size **about 1½ cups**   Prep Time **20 mins**   Pressure Time **4 mins**   Total Time **40 mins**

1 tsp avocado oil or olive oil

2 medium jalapeños, chopped (see Tip)

1 cup Chicken Bone Broth (page 44) or store-bought chicken broth

1 cup fresh riced cauliflower

2 tsp arrowroot starch, or cornstarch

1 tbsp water

2 tbsp cream cheese

¼ cup shredded Cheddar cheese

Salt, to taste

Black pepper, to taste

Chopped scallions, for garnish

For the sausage balls:
8oz (225g) ground pork

⅛ tsp garlic powder

⅛ tsp onion powder

¼ tsp dried thyme leaves

½ tsp fennel seed

¼ tsp salt

¼ tsp black pepper

1 tsp hot sauce

1. Prepare the sausage balls. In a medium bowl, mix together the ground pork, garlic powder, onion powder, thyme, fennel seed, salt, pepper, and hot sauce. (This is easiest when done by hand.) Roll the sausage into ½-inch (1.25cm) balls.

2. Select **Sauté (More),** and add the oil. When hot, arrange the sausage balls in a single layer. Allow the sausage to fry undisturbed for 4 minutes. Turn and fry for 2 minutes more. Push the sausage to the side of the inner pot. Add the jalapeños and sauté for 2 minutes more. Press **Cancel** to turn off Sauté.

3. Add the broth and riced cauliflower, and stir to combine. Lock the lid and set the steam release valve to the sealing position. Select **Pressure Cook (High),** and set the cook time for **4 minutes.**

4. Once the cook time is complete, allow the pressure to release naturally for 5 minutes, then quick release any remaining pressure.

5. In a small bowl, mix together the starch and 1 tablespoon water. Stir the mixture into the inner pot along with the cream cheese and Cheddar until melted and smooth. Season with salt and pepper to taste. Portion the soup into two serving bowls and garnish with scallions. Serve immediately.

TIP   If you prefer a milder soup, remove and discard the seeds from the jalapeños. If you like the heat turned up a notch, keep the seeds intact.

In a hurry? Take a shortcut by making this recipe with 8oz (225g) of your favorite pre-mixed sausage from the grocery store.

This recipe is very low in carbs as it is, but you can reduce them even further by omitting the arrowroot or cornstarch thickener.

NUTRITION PER SERVING:
Calories **445** • Total Fat **34.6g** • Total Carb **5g** • Fiber **2g** • Total Sugars **2g** • Protein **28g**

Harvest Apple Butternut Squash Soup

PROGRAM
**Sauté (More),
Pressure Cook (High)**

RELEASE
Natural and Quick

Gluten-Free, Dairy-Free, Vegan

Can a soup be described as "cozy"? With a kick of ginger and a hint of natural sweetness from the apple, this velvety soup is about as cozy as it gets! A mugful makes a wonderful afternoon pick-me-up.

Serves **2**   Serving Size **about 1½ cups**   Prep Time **15 mins**   Pressure Time **4 mins**   Total Time **30 mins**

1 tsp avocado oil or olive oil

¼ cup diced yellow onion

½ cup diced carrot (about 1 medium carrot)

1 clove garlic, minced

1 cup vegetable broth

10oz (285g) cubed butternut squash (about 1½ cups)

1 Fuji apple (or another sweet variety), cored and roughly chopped

¼ tsp ground sage

½ tsp ginger powder

¾ tsp salt

¼ tsp black pepper

1 bay leaf

¼ cup full-fat coconut milk

1. Select **Sauté (More)** and add the oil to the inner pot. When hot, add the onion and carrot, and sauté for 3 minutes. Add the garlic and sauté for 1 minute more.

2. Press **Cancel** to turn off Sauté. Stir in the vegetable broth, squash, apple, sage, ginger, salt, pepper, and bay leaf. Lock the lid and set the steam release valve to the sealing position. Select **Pressure Cook (High),** and set the cook time for **4 minutes.**

3. Once the cook time is complete, allow the pressure to release naturally for 5 minutes, then quick release any remaining pressure. Press **Cancel** to turn off Keep Warm.

4. Discard the bay leaf. Stir in the coconut milk. Working in batches if needed, transfer the soup to a blender (or use an immersion blender directly in the inner pot) and carefully blend until smooth. Serve immediately.

TIP   It doesn't have to be harvest time to enjoy this delicious soup. If squash isn't currently in season, use frozen butternut squash instead of fresh.

NUTRITION PER SERVING:
Calories **235** • Total Fat **8.8g** • Total Carb **40g** • Fiber **7g** • Total Sugars **17g** • Protein **3g**

Hungarian Mushroom Soup

Mushrooms are nutritional powerhouses that contain plenty of fiber and a lot of important nutrients such as B vitamins and selenium. This rich and creamy soup is a delicious way to get more of these healthy gems into your diet!

PROGRAM
Sauté (More), Pressure Cook (High)

RELEASE
Natural and Quick

Gluten-Free, Keto-Friendly Variation

Serves **2**   Serving Size **about 1½ cups**   Prep Time **15 mins**   Pressure Time **5 mins**   Total Time **35 mins**

1 tbsp salted butter

½ cup chopped yellow onion (about ½ small onion)

8oz (225g) sliced cremini mushrooms (about 3 cups)

1¼ cups Chicken Bone Broth (page 44) or store-bought chicken broth

1 tbsp tamari

1 tsp sweet Hungarian paprika

¼ tsp salt

¼ tsp black pepper

¼ cup half & half

2 tbsp arrowroot starch, or cornstarch

2 tbsp sour cream

1 tsp fresh lemon juice

2 tsp chopped dill

1. Select **Sauté (More),** and add the butter to the inner pot. When hot, add the onion and mushrooms, and sauté for 6 minutes.

2. Press **Cancel.** Stir in the chicken broth, tamari, paprika, salt, and pepper. Lock the lid and set the steam release valve to the sealing position. Select **Pressure Cook (High),** and set the cook time for **5 minutes.**

3. Once the cook time is complete, allow the pressure to release naturally for 5 minutes, then quick release any remaining pressure.

4. Press **Cancel** and select **Sauté (More).** In a small bowl, whisk together the half & half and the starch. Stir the mixture into the inner pot and bring just up to a simmer. Remove the inner pot from the base and stir in the sour cream and lemon juice.

5. Transfer the soup to a blender (or use an immersion blender directly in the inner pot), and pulse until the mushrooms are finely minced but not fully puréed. Stir in the dill and serve immediately.

TIP | Make it keto friendly: Omit the starch thickener. It will be thinner like a broth-based soup but will still have all of the delicious flavors.

NUTRITION PER SERVING:
Calories **249** • Total Fat **15.1g** • Total Carb **20g** • Fiber **3g** • Total Sugars **7g** • Protein **11g**

Sides and Veggies

Pot-in-Pot White Rice

PROGRAM
Pressure Cook (High)

RELEASE
Natural and Quick

Gluten-Free, Dairy-Free, Vegan

This rice is meant to be cooked at the same time as another dish, cutting your dinner prep time and allowing your whole meal to come out hot and ready to eat all at once. Master this simple trick, and dinner time will become a snap!

Serves **2**   Serving Size **1 cup**   Prep Time **2 mins**   Pressure Time **6 mins**   Total Time **20 mins**

1 cup white jasmine, white basmati, or long-grain white rice, rinsed

1 cup water

¼ tsp salt

1. Place an egg steamer trivet with 1½–2-inch (3.75–5cm) legs in the inner pot. If cooking the rice with another dish under the rice, the liquid from that dish will be enough to allow the Instant Pot to come up to pressure, so you do not need to add any additional water to the inner pot. If cooking without another dish under the rice, add 1 cup water to the inner pot.

2. To a round stainless steel pan, 6 inches (15.25cm) in diameter and no more than 2 inches (5cm) tall, add the rice, 1 cup water, and salt. Place the pan on the egg steamer trivet.

3. Lock the lid and set the steam release valve to the sealing position. Select **Pressure Cook (High),** and set the cook time for **6 minutes** (or the time specified in the recipe that is cooking in the inner pot underneath the rice, up to 25 minutes).

4. Once the cook time is complete, allow the pressure to release naturally for 5 minutes, then quick release any remaining pressure. Fluff the rice with a fork and serve immediately.

TIP

This recipe works with any dish that has a cook time between 6 and 25 minutes and that allows enough room for the rice to sit above the dish underneath. White rice cooked with the pot-in-pot method doesn't tend to overcook easily, so leaving it in the pot until the other dish is done is no problem.

If your egg steamer trivet comes with handles, fold them down before placing the pan on top.

To find a stainless steel pan in the right size for pot-in-pot cooking, look for a set of stackable pans made to fit in a 3-quart pressure cooker. The individual pans from these sets are typically 6 inches (15.25cm) in diameter and 2 inches (5cm) tall, which will work perfectly in the Instant Pot Mini for pot-in-pot cooking.

NUTRITION PER SERVING:
Calories **338** • Total Fat **0.6g** • Total Carb **74g** • Fiber **1g** • Total Sugars **0g** • Protein **7g**

Fluffy Brown Rice

You'll probably find yourself coming back to this staple recipe over and over again. This no-nonsense, whole-grain side dish makes an ideal base for curries, stir-fries, burrito bowls, and so much more.

PROGRAM
Pressure Cook (High)

RELEASE
Natural and Quick

Gluten-Free, Dairy-Free, Vegan

Serves **2**   Serving Size **about 1 cup**   Prep Time **2 mins**   Pressure Time **23 mins**   Total Time **45 mins**

¾ cup long-grain brown rice

2½ cups water

½ tsp salt

1 tsp avocado oil or olive oil

1. Add the rice, 2½ cups water, salt, and oil to the inner pot. Lock the lid and set the steam release valve to the sealing position. Select **Pressure Cook (High),** and set the cook time for **23 minutes.**

2. Once the cook time is complete, allow the pressure to release naturally for 15 minutes, then quick release any remaining pressure.

3. Use a fine-mesh strainer to drain the excess water. Transfer the rice to a serving dish and serve immediately.

TIP | The additional step of cooking with extra water then draining gives this rice its fluffy texture. Draining the water at the end takes away any sticky, excess starch and leaves behind just fluffy and delicious brown rice.

NUTRITION PER SERVING:

Calories **274** • Total Fat **4.5g** • Total Carb **53g** • Fiber **3g** • Total Sugars **0g** • Protein **5g**

Quick Cauliflower Rice

This supremely simple recipe cooks up very fast. It will give your meal an extra serving of veggies and serve as a nearly carb-free bed for countless creamy sauces and meaty stews.

PROGRAM
Pressure Cooke (Low)

RELEASE
Quick

Gluten-Free, Dairy-Free, Keto Friendly, Vegan

Serves **2**   Serving Size **about 1 cup**   Prep Time **1 min**   Pressure Time **3 mins**   Total Time **15 mins**

2 cups fresh shredded (riced) cauliflower

1 tsp olive oil

Salt, to taste

Black pepper, to taste

1. Place a steamer basket with feet in the inner pot and add 1 cup water. Add the cauliflower to the steamer basket. Lock the lid and set the steam release valve to the sealing position. Select **Pressure Cook (Low),** and set the cook time for **3 minutes.**

2. Once the cook time is complete, quick release the pressure. Remove the steamer basket immediately to avoid overcooking. Transfer the cauliflower rice to a serving dish, toss with the olive oil, and season to taste with salt and pepper. Serve immediately.

TIP   Frozen riced cauliflower works as well. However, this product tends to cook up faster and lose more of its volume when cooking, so increase the amount of cauliflower rice to 3 cups and reduce the cook time to 2 minutes.

Fresh riced cauliflower is very easy and frugal to make at home. Simply shred a head of cauliflower on a cheese grater.

This cauliflower rice makes a great base for many dishes, such as Tangy Beef and Broccoli (page 59), Thai Peanut Pork Curry (page 71), and Orange Marmalade Chicken (page 60).

NUTRITION PER SERVING:
Calories **40** • Total Fat **2.3g** • Total Carb **4g** • Fiber **2g** • Total Sugars **2g** • Protein **2g**

Quinoa in a Snap

Quinoa has a delicious nutty flavor and is a great way to add some variety to your diet. Sprinkle on a salad, stir into soup, use in place of rice in burrito bowls, or use as the base to a stir-fry.

PROGRAM
**Sauté (More),
Pressure Cook (Low)**

RELEASE
Natural and Quick

Gluten-Free, Dairy-Free, Vegan

Serves **2**   Serving Size **about 1 cup**   Prep Time **5 mins**   Pressure Time **2 mins**   Total Time **20 mins**

1¼ cups water

½ tsp salt

½ tsp avocado oil or olive oil (optional)

¾ cup quinoa

1. Select **Sauté (More).** Add 1¼ cups water, salt, and oil (if using) to the inner pot, and bring up to a simmer.

2. Add the quinoa and press **Cancel.** Lock the lid and set the steam release valve to the sealing position. Select **Pressure Cook (Low),** and set the cook time for **2 minutes.**

3. Once the cook time is complete, allow the pressure to release naturally for 5 minutes, then quick release any remaining pressure. Fluff with a fork and serve immediately.

TIP   Check your package of quinoa to see if it is prewashed. If it is not, rinse it well with a fine-mesh strainer before cooking to remove the bitter, naturally occurring saponins.

The extra step of bringing the water to a boil before adding the quinoa keeps the finished product from being mushy and prevents the quinoa seeds from sticking together in clumps. If you are in a hurry, you can skip this step.

For savory quinoa, substitute broth for the water. Chicken Bone Broth (page 44) or vegetable broth will give your quinoa delicious flavor.

Cooked quinoa stores well in the refrigerator and makes for easy meals later on. Use up leftover quinoa within 5 days, or freeze individual portions in freezer-safe containers or freezer bags for longer storage.

NUTRITION PER SERVING:
Calories **245** • Total Fat **5g** • Total Carb **41g** • Fiber **4g** • Total Sugars **0g** • Protein **9g**

Kimchi Fried Rice

Kimchi offers a melody of exotic flavors, and this recipe highlights them all. By waiting until the end of the cooking time to mix the kimchi into the rice, you help to preserve its powerful probiotic benefits as well!

PROGRAM
**Sauté (More),
Pressure Cook (High)**

RELEASE
Natural and Quick

**Gluten-Free,
Dairy-Free**

Serves **2**   Serving Size **1 cup**   Prep Time **8 mins**   Pressure Time **4 mins**   Total Time **25 mins**

1 tbsp avocado oil or olive oil

¾ cup white jasmine rice, rinsed

1 large egg, lightly beaten

¾ cup water

2 tbsp kimchi juice

1 tbsp tamari

1 tsp toasted sesame oil

1 tbsp gochujang sauce (Korean fermented chili paste)

¼ cup kimchi, roughly chopped

For serving:
Toasted sesame seeds

Thinly sliced nori

Chopped scallions

Pickled ginger

1. Select **Sauté (More),** and heat the oil in the inner pot. In a small bowl, mix the jasmine rice with the egg. Once the oil is hot, add the rice and egg mixture to the inner pot. Fry the rice, stirring constantly, for about 3 minutes, or until the egg has cooked through and the rice appears dry and crumbly. (Stirring constantly keeps the egg from cooking into clumps and allows the rice grains to be individually coated in egg.)

2. Press **Cancel.** Add ¾ cup water, kimchi juice, tamari, and sesame oil. Lock the lid and set the steam release valve to the sealing position. Select **Pressure Cook (High),** and set the cook time for **4 minutes.**

3. Once the cook time is complete, allow the pressure to release naturally for 5 minutes, then quick release any remaining pressure. Stir in the gochujang sauce and kimchi. Portion the fried rice into two serving dishes, and garnish with toasted sesame seeds, nori, scallions, and pickled ginger. Serve immediately.

TIP | Many traditional fried rice recipes call for driedout, day-old rice in order to keep the finished dish from becoming mushy. In this recipe, the technique of stir-frying the uncooked rice in a scrambled egg before adding water helps the rice stay dry and delivers a classic fried rice texture fresh out of the Instant Pot.

Make this side dish into a light meal by topping with a sunny-side up or fried egg.

Gochujang sauce can often be found in the Asian or international foods section in the grocery store. Substitute with Sriracha sauce if desired.

Kimchi is a delicious fermented cabbage condiment and can often be found in the refrigerated section of the grocery store.

NUTRITION PER SERVING (EXCLUDING OPTIONS FOR SERVING):
Calories **383** • Total Fat **12.2g** • Total Carb **57g** • Fiber **1g** • Total Sugars **1g** • Protein **9g**

Curried Cauliflower with Raisins and Almonds

Crisp almonds and plump golden raisins elevate humble cauliflower in this savory side dish. A sauce made of vibrant curry flavors and rich coconut milk thickens to bring all of the elements of this dish together.

PROGRAM
**Sauté (More),
Pressure Cook (Low)**

RELEASE
Quick

Gluten-Free, Dairy-Free, Keto-Friendly Variation, Vegan

Serves **2**   Serving Size **about 1 cup**   Prep Time **10 mins**   Pressure Time **0 mins**   Total Time **25 mins**

2 tbsp sliced raw almonds

10oz (285g) cauliflower florets (about 3 cups)

2 tbsp golden raisins

For the sauce:

⅓ cup full-fat coconut milk

1 tsp curry powder

⅛ tsp garlic powder

½ tsp salt

⅛ tsp black pepper

½ tsp arrowroot starch, or cornstarch

1. Select **Sauté (More).** When hot, add the almonds and dry toast for about 4 minutes, stirring often, until they are lightly browned. Remove the toasted almonds from the inner pot and set aside. Press **Cancel.**

2. Place a steamer basket with feet in the inner pot and add 1 cup water. Add the cauliflower to the steamer basket. Lock the lid and set the steam release valve to the sealing position. Select **Pressure Cook (Low),** and set the cook time for **0 minutes.**

3. While the cauliflower is cooking, prepare the sauce. In a small bowl, whisk together the coconut milk, curry powder, garlic powder, salt, pepper, and starch.

4. Once the cook time is complete, quick release the pressure and press **Cancel.** Remove the steamer basket from the inner pot. Discard the water and replace the inner pot.

5. Select **Sauté (More).** Add the sauce to the inner pot. Cook and stir until the sauce thickens, about 1 minute.

6. Add the steamed cauliflower and the raisins, and toss gently to coat in the sauce. Transfer to a serving bowl and sprinkle with the toasted almonds. Serve immediately.

TIP | Vegetables can overcook easily under pressure. Using a 0-minute cook time on low pressure is a great way to perfectly cook delicate vegetables without letting them turn to mush.

If you cannot locate golden raisins, substitute with regular brown raisins.

Make it keto friendly: Omit the raisins.

NUTRITION PER SERVING:

Calories **245** • Total Fat **16.6g** • Total Carb **21g** • Fiber **7g** • Total Sugars **10g** • Protein **9g**

Cranberry Apple Quinoa Pilaf

This pilaf is perfect for fall and could even serve as a vegan substitute for Thanksgiving stuffing. The fresh herbs and garlic and the balance of sweet and tart from the apples and cranberries come together beautifully in this harvest-time side dish.

PROGRAM
**Sauté (More),
Pressure Cook (Low)**

RELEASE
Natural and Quick

Gluten-Free, Dairy-Free, Vegan

Serves **2**   Serving Size **1 cup**   Prep Time **15 mins**   Pressure Time **2 mins**   Total Time **35 mins**

1 tbsp chopped raw pecan halves

1 tsp avocado oil or olive oil

¼ cup minced red onion

1 clove garlic, minced

1 tsp fresh thyme leaves

1 tsp chopped sage

1 cup vegetable broth

¼ cup apple cider or apple juice

½ cup cored and finely chopped Gala apple (or another sweet variety; peeled, if desired)

¼ cup cranberries (fresh or frozen)

½ tsp salt

¼ tsp black pepper

¾ cup quinoa

2 tbsp chopped parsley

1. Select **Sauté (More).** When hot, add the pecans and dry toast for about 5 minutes, stirring often, until they are lightly browned. Remove the toasted pecans from the inner pot and set aside.

2. Add the oil to the inner pot. When hot, add the red onion and sauté for 2 minutes. Add the garlic, thyme, and sage, and sauté for 1 minute more.

3. Add the broth, apple cider, apple, cranberries, salt, and pepper. Bring up to a simmer, then stir in the quinoa. Press **Cancel.**

4. Lock the lid and set the steam release valve to the sealing position. Select **Pressure Cook (Low),** and set the cook time for **2 minutes.**

5. Once the cook time is complete, allow the pressure to release naturally for 5 minutes, then quick release any remaining pressure.

6. Fluff the pilaf with a fork to allow any residual liquid to absorb. Stir in the parsley and transfer to a serving bowl. Sprinkle with the toasted pecans and serve immediately.

TIP

Check your package of quinoa to see if it is prewashed. If it is not, make sure to rinse it well in a fine-mesh strainer before cooking to remove the bitter, naturally occurring saponins.

If you do not have fresh or frozen cranberries, dried cranberries can be substituted. Stir them in at the end of cook time along with the parsley.

Try this pilaf alongside the Cranberry Chicken on page 53 or the Cinnamon Apple Pork Tenderloin on page 54.

NUTRITION PER SERVING:
Calories **329** • Total Fat **8.5g** • Total Carb **51g** • Fiber **7g** • Total Sugars **8g** • Protein **10g**

Lemony Cauliflower Tabbouleh

This light salad is filled with a rainbow of colors and equally vibrant flavors. It's perfectly refreshing and sure to brighten up your plate as well as help you avoid the gluten and excess carbs that come with traditional tabbouleh.

PROGRAM
Pressure Cook (Low)

RELEASE
Quick

Gluten-Free, Dairy-Free, Keto Friendly, Vegan

Serves **2**   Serving Size **about 1 cup**   Prep Time **5 mins**   Pressure Time **0 mins**   Total Time **50 mins**

½ cup fresh riced cauliflower

1 cup finely chopped parsley

½ cup finely diced cucumber

¼ cup finely diced tomato

2 tbsp finely diced red onion

3 mint leaves, finely chopped

¼ tsp salt

1 tbsp lemon juice

1 tbsp olive oil

Lemon zest, for garnish

1. Place a steamer basket with feet in the inner pot and add 1 cup water. Add the riced cauliflower to the steamer basket. Lock the lid and set the steam release valve to the sealing position. Select **Pressure Cook (Low)**, and set the cook time for **0 minutes.**

2. Once the cook time is complete, quick release the pressure and remove the steamer basket. In a shallow dish, spread the cooked cauliflower in a thin layer. Refrigerate until completely cooled, about 15 minutes.

3. While the cauliflower chills, in a medium bowl, combine the parsley, cucumber, tomato, red onion, mint, salt, lemon juice, and olive oil.

4. Add the cooled cauliflower to the parsley mixture, and toss to combine. Cover and refrigerate for at least 20 minutes to allow the flavors to blend. Top with lemon zest and serve.

TIP | Looking to add some healthy carbs to your diet? For a delicious, starchy side, try this recipe with cooked quinoa instead of cauliflower.

Fresh riced cauliflower is very easy and frugal to make at home. Simply shred a head of cauliflower on a cheese grater.

NUTRITION PER SERVING:
Calories **88** • Total Fat **7.1g** • Total Carb **6g** • Fiber **2g** • Total Sugars **2g** • Protein **2g**

Cut-the-Carbs Spaghetti Squash

This light and healthy pasta substitute is ready to soak up whatever rich and savory sauce you are serving. It will take your dinner's carb load down drastically while still providing a delicious base for your meal.

PROGRAM
Pressure Cook (High)

RELEASE
Quick

Gluten-Free, Dairy-Free, Keto Friendly, Vegan

Serves **2**   Serving Size **about 1 cup squash**   Prep Time **5 mins**   Pressure Time **12 mins**   Total Time **25 mins**

1 small spaghetti squash (1¼–1½lb; 570–680g)

1 tbsp olive oil

Salt, to taste

Black pepper, to taste

1. Rinse the outside of the spaghetti squash and slice in half lengthwise. Scoop out the seeds and discard.

2. Place the steam rack in the inner pot and add 1 cup water. Place the squash halves on the steam rack. Lock the lid and set the steam release valve to the sealing position. Select **Pressure Cook (High),** and set the cook time for **12 minutes.**

3. Once the cook time is complete, quick release the pressure. Carefully remove the squash halves from the inner pot with tongs. Drizzle the squash halves with the olive oil, and season with salt and pepper to taste. Fluff the squash "noodles" with a fork and scoop out into a serving dish, or use the squash shells as bowls. Top as desired and serve immediately.

TIP | If you can't find a small enough spaghetti squash, cut a larger one into quarters and cook two quarters at a time. Once cooled, you can transfer any leftovers to a freezer-safe container or bag and freeze for another meal.

NUTRITION PER SERVING:
Calories **101** • Total Fat **8.4g** • Total Carb **10g** • Fiber **2g** • Total Sugars **4g** • Protein **1g**

Tuscan Polenta

Garlic, sun-dried tomatoes, Parmesan, and fresh basil give this golden polenta its Tuscan twist. This side dish is rich and satisfying and makes a perfect accompaniment to light proteins such as grilled fish or chicken.

PROGRAM
**Sauté (More),
Pressure Cook (High)**

RELEASE
Natural and Quick

Gluten-Free, Dairy-Free Variation, Vegan Variation

Serves **2**   Serving Size **about ½ cup**   Prep Time **5 mins**   Pressure Time **8 mins**   Total Time **25 mins**

1 tbsp olive oil

1 tbsp thinly sliced sun-dried tomato halves

2 cloves garlic, minced

1⅓ cups Chicken Bone Broth (page 44) or store-bought chicken broth

⅓ cup dry coarsely ground corn grits (also called *polenta*, not quick grits)

½ tsp dried oregano

½ tsp salt

3 tbsp chopped basil (loosely packed)

2 tbsp shredded Parmesan cheese

1. Select **Sauté (More),** and add the oil to the inner pot. When hot, add the sun-dried tomatoes and garlic, and sauté for 1 minute.

2. Press **Cancel** and stir in the broth, scraping the bottom of the pot to remove any stuck-on bits. Stir in the grits, oregano, and salt.

3. Lock the lid and set the steam release valve to the sealing position. Select **Pressure Cook (High),** and set the cook time for **8 minutes.**

4. Once the cook time is complete, allow the pressure to release naturally for 5 minutes, then quick release any remaining pressure.

5. Stir in the basil and Parmesan, and serve immediately.

TIP | Make it dairy-free and vegan: Substitute vegetable broth for the chicken bone broth. Omit the Parmesan, or substitute with a vegan Parmesan alternative.

Very coarsely ground grits work the best for this recipe. Finely ground cornmeal can become too thick and scorch on the bottom of the inner pot, causing a Burn error message. If your grits are a finer grind, add an additional ½ cup water.

NUTRITION PER SERVING:
Calories **198** • Total Fat **8.9g** • Total Carb **23g** • Fiber **3g** • Total Sugars **1g** • Protein **8g**

Lemon Dill Creamer Potatoes

Lemon and dill combine beautifully in this recipe to give these delicate baby potatoes a burst of flavor. With crispy skins and delightfully fluffy middles, this plant-based side dish will make a perfect accompaniment to your meal.

PROGRAM
Pressure Cook (High), Sauté (More)

RELEASE
Quick

Gluten-Free, Dairy-Free Variation, Vegan Variation

Serves **2**   Serving Size **about 1 cup**   Prep Time **5 mins**   Pressure Time **6 mins**   Total Time **35 mins**

1lb (450g) creamer potatoes, 1–1½in (2.5–3.75cm) in diameter

1 tbsp avocado oil or olive oil

1 tbsp salted butter

1 tbsp fresh lemon juice

½ tsp lemon zest

1 tbsp chopped dill

1 tsp flaky sea salt

1. Place a steamer basket with feet in the inner pot and add 1 cup water. Add the potatoes to the steamer basket. Lock the lid and set the steam release valve to the sealing position. Select **Pressure Cook (High),** and set the cook time for **6 minutes.**

2. Once the cook time is complete, quick release the pressure and press **Cancel** to turn off Keep Warm. Remove the steamer basket and set aside. Discard the water from the inner pot. Replace the inner pot and select **Sauté (More).**

3. Add the oil and heat until it begins to shimmer. Add the steamed potatoes in a single layer. Allow to cook, undisturbed, for 5 minutes. Stir and cook for 5 minutes more.

4. Add the butter, lemon juice, lemon zest, dill, and salt, and cook just until the butter is melted. Toss to coat the potatoes, and remove the inner pot from the base. Serve immediately.

TIP | Make it dairy-free and vegan: Substitute your favorite vegan spread for the butter.

NUTRITION PER SERVING:
Calories **289** • Total Fat **13g** • Total Carb **40g** • Fiber **5g** • Total Sugars **2g** • Protein **2g**

Easy Potato Cauliflower Mash

This recipe is a great way to sneak in an extra serving of vegetables. The potatoes and cauliflower cook up so quickly and are mashed together right in the inner pot with no draining necessary.

PROGRAM
Pressure Cook (High)

RELEASE
Quick

Gluten-Free, Dairy-Free Variation, Vegan Variation, Keto-Friendly Variation

Serves **2**   Serving Size **about 1 cup**   Prep Time **5 mins**   Pressure Time **4 mins**   Total Time **20 mins**

8oz (255g) red potatoes, peeled if desired, and cut into ½in (1.25cm) cubes (about 2 medium potatoes)

8oz (255g) cauliflower florets (about ½ small head)

½ cup vegetable broth or Chicken Bone Broth (page 44)

⅛ tsp smoked paprika

¼ tsp garlic powder

½ tsp salt

⅛ tsp black pepper

2 tbsp cream cheese

Chopped chives (optional), for garnish

1. To the inner pot, add the potatoes, cauliflower, broth, paprika, garlic powder, salt, and pepper.

2. Lock the lid and set the steam release valve to the sealing position. Select **Pressure Cook (High),** and set the cook time for **4 minutes.**

3. Once the cook time is complete, quick release the pressure. Add the cream cheese. Using a potato masher, mash the mixture until nearly smooth (some lumps will remain).

4. Top with chopped chives, if desired, and serve immediately.

TIP | Use this mash as a side dish anywhere you would normally serve mashed potatoes. Try it alongside Bacon and Mushroom Covered Pork Chops (page 55) or as a base for Classic Beef Stroganoff (page 75).

Make it dairy-free and vegan: Use vegetable broth and substitute the cream cheese with 2 teaspoons olive oil.

Make it keto friendly: Use an additional 8oz (255g) cauliflower florets instead of the potatoes. Reduce the broth to ¼ cup.

NUTRITION PER SERVING:
Calories **172** • Total Fat **5.1g** • Total Carb **29g** • Fiber **5g** • Total Sugars **5g** • Protein **6g**

No-Fuss Black Beans

It doesn't get much simpler or more versatile than this black bean recipe. Transform nutritionally dense dry beans into a piping hot, vegan side dish in less than an hour. No soaking, can opener, or fuss required!

PROGRAM
Bean/Chili (High)

RELEASE
Natural and Quick

Gluten-Free, Dairy-Free, Vegan

Serves **2**   Serving Size **about ½ cup**   Prep Time **2 mins**   Pressure Time **25 mins**   Total Time **42 mins**

½ cup dry black beans, rinsed
1½ cups water
½ tsp salt

1. Add the black beans, 1½ cups water, and salt to the inner pot. Lock the lid and set the steam release valve to the sealing position. Select **Bean/Chili (High),** and set the cook time for **25 minutes.**

2. Once the cook time is complete, allow the pressure to release naturally for 10 minutes, then quick release any remaining pressure. Drain if desired and serve immediately.

TIP | Spice it up by adding 1 teaspoon of your favorite taco seasoning blend before cooking.

NUTRITION PER SERVING:
Calories **165** • Total Fat **0.7g** • Total Carb **30g** • Fiber **8g** • Total Sugars **1g** • Protein **10g**

Soy Ginger–Glazed Carrots

These salty, sweet baby carrots are a delicious way to get an extra veggie serving onto your plate! All of the flavors come together with a pop and make a perfect accompaniment to any Asian-inspired main dish.

PROGRAM
Pressure Cook (High), Sauté (Normal)

RELEASE
Quick

Gluten-Free, Dairy-Free, Vegan

Serves **2**   Serving Size **about 1 cup**   Prep Time **5 mins**   Pressure Time **5 mins**   Total Time **25 mins**

8oz (225g) baby carrots, about ½in (1.25cm) in diameter

½in (1.25cm) piece fresh ginger, minced

1 tsp avocado oil or olive oil

Chopped scallions, for garnish

For the glaze:
2 tbsp tamari

1 tsp toasted sesame oil

1 tsp rice vinegar

Dash of garlic powder

Dash of red pepper flakes

2 tsp coconut sugar

½ tsp arrowroot starch, or cornstarch

1. Place a steamer basket with feet in the inner pot and add 1 cup water. Add the carrots to the steamer basket and sprinkle with the ginger. Lock the lid and set the steam release valve to the sealing position. Select **Pressure Cook (High),** and set the cook time for **5 minutes.**

2. While the carrots are cooking, prepare the glaze. In as small bowl, combine the tamari, sesame oil, rice vinegar, garlic powder, red pepper flakes, coconut sugar, and arrowroot starch. Set aside.

3. Once the cook time is complete, quick release the pressure and press **Cancel** to turn off Keep Warm. Remove the steamer basket and set aside. Discard the water from the inner pot and place it back in the Instant Pot. Select **Sauté (Normal).**

4. Add the oil to the inner pot and heat until it begins to shimmer. Add the carrots and ginger, and sauté for 3 minutes. Pour in the glaze. Cook and stir until thick and bubbly and the carrots are fully glazed, about 1 minute. Place on a serving dish and garnish with chopped scallions. Serve immediately.

TIP | Cook time in this recipe depends on the diameter of your baby carrots. If they're more than ½ inch (1.25cm) in diameter, add 1 minute to the cook time. If they are less, reduce the cook time by 1 minute.

NUTRITION PER SERVING:
Calories **103** • Total Fat **4.7g** • Total Carb **14g** • Fiber **3g** • Total Sugars **9g** • Protein **3g**

Artichokes with Garlic-Herb Butter

PROGRAM
Pressure Cook (High)

RELEASE
Natural and Quick

Gluten-Free, Dairy-Free Variation, Keto Friendly, Vegan Variation

Artichokes steam up quickly and easily in the Instant Pot and make for a fun and unique side dish that is also very low in carbs. It could be argued, though, that the artichoke just serves as a delivery system for the fragrant garlic-herb butter!

Makes **2 small artichokes**   Serving Size **1 small artichoke**   Prep Time **5 mins**   Pressure Time **14 mins**   Total Time **35 mins**

2 small artichokes, 6–8oz (170–225g) each

2 tbsp salted butter

1 clove garlic, minced

½ tsp fresh thyme leaves

½ tsp finely chopped fresh rosemary

¼ tsp salt

1. Wash the artichokes and trim the stems down to 1 inch (2.5cm). Slice 1 inch (2.5cm) off the tips of the artichokes.

2. Place the steam rack in the inner pot and add 1 cup water. Place the artichokes stem-side down on the steam rack.

3. To a lidded 4fl oz (120ml) canning jar, add the butter, garlic, thyme, rosemary, and salt. Place the jar on the steam rack next to the artichokes. Rest the flat canning lid on top to keep out excess moisture. (There is no need to screw on the ring.)

4. Lock the lid and set the steam release valve to the sealing position. Select **Pressure Cook (High),** and set the cook time for **14 minutes.**

5. Once the cook time is complete, allow the pressure to release naturally for 5 minutes, then quick release any remaining pressure.

6. Using tongs, carefully move the artichokes and canning jar to a serving tray. Remove the lid from the jar. Serve when the artichokes are cool enough to handle, about 5 minutes. To eat, remove the artichoke petals one at a time and dip the base in the garlic-herb butter. Only the soft white part at the base of each petal is edible. Scrape the white portion off with your front teeth and discard the rest of the petal. Be sure to discard the inedible fuzzy purple and white "choke" from the center of the artichoke. The solid base below the choke is the artichoke heart, which is edible and delicious.

TIP | Make it dairy-free and vegan: Substitute olive oil for the butter.

NUTRITION PER SERVING:
Calories **153** • Total Fat **11.1g** • Total Carb **12g** • Fiber **5.7g** • Total Sugars **1g** • Protein **3g**

Maple-Glazed Brussels Sprouts

These little green nuggets of sweetness will melt in your mouth. The Instant Pot pressure cooks them with steam until they're perfectly tender and then crisps them up using the Sauté setting. They're finished off with a sticky maple glaze.

PROGRAM
Pressure Cook (High), Sauté (More)

RELEASE
Quick

Gluten-Free, Dairy-Free, Vegan

Serves **2**   Serving Size **about 1 cup**   Prep Time **5 mins**   Pressure Time **5 mins**   Total Time **35 mins**

10oz (285g) Brussels sprouts (about 2 cups), 1in (2.5cm) in diameter, washed and trimmed

1 tbsp avocado oil or olive oil

For the sauce:
2 tbsp pure maple syrup

1 tsp Dijon mustard

1 tbsp balsamic vinegar

¼ tsp dried thyme leaves

½ tsp salt

¼ tsp black pepper

½ tsp arrowroot starch, or cornstarch

1. Place a steamer basket with feet in the inner pot and add 1 cup water. Add the Brussels sprouts to the steamer basket. Lock the lid and set the steam release valve to the sealing position. Select **Pressure Cook (High)**, and set the cook time for **5 minutes.**

2. While the Brussels sprouts are cooking, prepare the sauce. In a small bowl, combine the maple syrup, Dijon mustard, balsamic vinegar, thyme, salt, pepper, and starch. Set aside.

3. Once the cook time is complete, quick release the pressure and press **Cancel** to turn off Keep Warm. Remove the steamer basket from the inner pot and set aside. Discard the water and replace the inner pot. Select **Sauté (More).**

4. Add the oil to the inner pot and heat until it begins to shimmer. Add the steamed Brussels sprouts to the inner pot in a single layer. Sauté undisturbed for 4 minutes. Stir and sauté for 3 minutes more.

5. Add the sauce to the Brussels sprouts. Stir and cook until the sauce thickens and the Brussels sprouts are fully coated, about 1 minute. Remove the inner pot from the base and serve immediately.

TIP | The cook time depends on the size of the Brussels sprouts. If your sprouts are bigger than 1 inch (2.5cm) in diameter, add 1 minute more to the cook time. If they're smaller, reduce the cook time by 1 minute.

NUTRITION PER SERVING:
Calories **190** • Total Fat **7.5g** • Total Carb **29g** • Fiber **6g** • Total Sugars **16g** • Protein **5g**

Parmesan Green Beans with Bacon

PROGRAM
**Pressure Cook (High),
Sauté (More)**

RELEASE
Quick

**Gluten-Free,
Keto Friendly**

The flavor combination found in this recipe is hard to beat. Savory Parmesan and salty bacon make this veggie side dish feel so indulgent that you'll have to remind yourself that it's also extremely low in carbs.

Serves **2**   Serving Size **about 1 cup**   Prep Time **5 mins**   Pressure Time **1 min**   Total Time **25 mins**

½lb (225g) green beans, washed and trimmed

2 slices uncooked bacon, chopped

⅛ tsp salt

⅛ tsp black pepper

Dash of garlic powder

Dash of onion powder

Dash of red pepper flakes

2 tbsp shredded Parmesan cheese

1. Place a steamer basket with feet in the inner pot and add 1 cup water. Add the green beans to the steamer basket. Lock the lid and set the steam release valve to the sealing position. Select **Pressure Cook (High),** and set the cook time for **1 minute.**

2. Once the cook time is complete, quick release the pressure. Press **Cancel** to turn off Keep Warm. Remove the steamer basket and set aside. Discard the water from the inner pot, and place it back in the Instant Pot. Select **Sauté (More).**

3. Once the pot is hot, add the bacon. Sauté until browned and crispy. With a slotted spoon, transfer the bacon to a paper towel–lined plate to drain, leaving behind the rendered bacon fat. Set the bacon aside.

4. Add the steamed green beans to the inner pot and allow to cook, undisturbed, for 3 minutes. Stir and cook for 2 minutes more. Add the salt, pepper, garlic powder, onion powder, and red pepper flakes, and sauté for 1 minute more.

5. Transfer the green beans to a serving dish and sprinkle with the Parmesan and bacon. Serve immediately.

TIP | The beans in this recipe are cooked so that they still have a nice crisp to them. If you like your green beans very soft, increase the cook time to 2 minutes.

NUTRITION PER SERVING:
Calories **222** • Total Fat **18.1g** • Total Carb **9g** • Fiber **3g** • Total Sugars **4g** • Protein **8g**

Sweet and Sour Danish Cabbage

This is a take on a simple dish that is traditionally served at Christmastime in Denmark. With deep purple cabbage cooked down in tangy apple cider vinegar and a touch of sweetness, this side dish adds vibrancy to the meal in both color and flavor.

PROGRAM
Pressure Cook (High)

RELEASE
Natural and Quick

Gluten-Free, Keto-Friendly Variation

Serves **2**   Serving Size **about 1 cup**   Prep Time **5 mins**   Pressure Time **5 mins**   Total Time **25 mins**

3 cups shredded red cabbage

½ tsp salt

¼ cup apple cider vinegar

1 tbsp salted butter

2 tbsp granulated sugar

1. To the inner pot, add the cabbage, salt, and apple cider vinegar. Place the butter on top of the mixture, and sprinkle the mixture with the sugar. Do not stir.

2. Lock the lid and set the steam release valve to the sealing position. Select **Pressure Cook (High),** and set the cook time for **5 minutes.**

3. Once the cook time is complete, allow the pressure to release naturally for 5 minutes, then quick release any remaining pressure.

4. Transfer to a serving bowl, discarding any excess liquid, and serve immediately.

TIP   Pair this side dish with the Bacon and Mushroom Covered Pork Chops on page 55 or the Cinnamon Apple Pork Tenderloin on page 54.

Make it keto friendly: Substitute your favorite sugar-free granulated sweetener for the sugar.

NUTRITION PER SERVING:
Calories **136** • Total Fat **5.7g** • Total Carb **21g** • Fiber **2g** • Total Sugars **17g** • Protein **2g**

Cornbread Bundtlet

This adorable, gluten-free Bundtlet makes a great addition to many so many dishes. Try it alongside Autumn Pumpkin Chili (page 78), or enjoy a slice with a smear of butter and a drizzle of honey.

PROGRAM
Pressure Cook (High)

RELEASE
Natural and Quick

Gluten-Free

Serves **6**   Serving Size **⅙ Bundtlet**   Prep Time **10 mins**   Pressure Time **25 mins**   Total Time **1 hour 15 mins**

½ cup (64g) cassava flour

½ cup (76g) medium-grind yellow or white cornmeal

1 tsp baking soda

½ tsp salt

3 tbsp salted butter, melted

¾ cup buttermilk

2 tbsp coconut sugar

1 large egg

1. In a medium bowl, mix together the cassava flour, cornmeal, baking soda, and salt. In a small bowl, whisk together the melted butter, buttermilk, coconut sugar, and egg. Add the buttermilk mixture to the flour mixture, and stir gently until just combined.

2. Spray a 3-cup Bundt pan with nonstick spray. Gently pour in the batter and carefully spread it out evenly. Place the steam rack in the inner pot and add 1 cup water. Place the pan on the steam rack. Lock the lid and set the steam release valve to the sealing position. Select **Pressure Cook (High),** and set the cook time for **25 minutes.**

3. Once the cook time is complete, allow the pressure to release naturally for 5 minutes, then quick release any remaining pressure. Carefully remove the lid so as not to let the condensation fall directly onto the cornbread.

4. Allow the cornbread to cool in the Bundt pan on a wire rack for 10 minutes. Then use a butter knife to loosen up the edges if necessary, and turn the cornbread out onto the wire rack to cool for at least 15 minutes more. Serve warm. Store leftovers in an airtight container at room temperature and use within 2 days. Reheat the cornbread in the microwave for a few seconds before serving.

TIP | For best results, use a food scale to accurately measure flours. If you do not have a food scale, gently spoon the flour into your measuring cup so as not to compact it. Inaccurately measuring flour can leave you with a hard and dense finished product.

NUTRITION PER SERVING:
Calories **165** • Total Fat **7.9g** • Total Carb **22g** • Fiber **2g** • Total Sugars **5g** • Protein **3g**

Snacks
and
Appetizers

Pickled Jalapeño Deviled Eggs

Perfect for a summer picnic or a low-carb appetizer, these deviled eggs take it to the next level with a hint of heat from the jalapeños. With the Instant Pot, cooking and preparing deviled eggs has never been easier!

PROGRAM
Pressure Cook (High)

RELEASE
Quick

**Gluten-Free,
Keto Friendly**

Serves **2**   Serving Size **3 egg halves**   Prep Time **5 mins**   Pressure Time **6 mins**   Total Time **25 mins**

3 large eggs

1 tbsp cream cheese

2 tbsp minced pickled jalapeños

1 tbsp pickled jalapeño juice

1 tsp spicy brown mustard

¼ tsp salt

Chipotle powder, for garnish

1. Place a steamer basket with feet in the inner pot and add 1 cup water. Add the eggs to the steamer basket. Lock the lid and set the steam release valve to the sealing position. Select **Pressure Cook (High),** and set the cook time for **6 minutes.**

2. Meanwhile, in a small bowl, combine the cream cheese, pickled jalapeños, pickled jalapeño juice, spicy brown mustard, and salt. Fill a small bowl with ice water.

3. Once the cook time is complete, quick release the pressure and immediately transfer the eggs to the bowl of ice water. Allow the eggs to cool in the ice water for 5 minutes. Drain the water and ice, and peel away the eggshells.

4. Cut the eggs in half lengthwise, and scoop the yolks into the cream cheese mixture. Mash the yolks and mix until smooth. Scoop the filling into the empty egg whites. Top each deviled egg with a sprinkle of chipotle powder. Arrange on a platter and chill until ready to serve.

TIP | A secret weapon for creating perfect deviled eggs in the Instant Pot is an egg steamer trivet. This cookware has holes designed to keep the eggs standing up while cooking, creating perfectly centered yolks every time. Egg steamer trivets are easily found online (page 13).

NUTRITION PER SERVING:

Calories **147** • Total Fat **11.1g** • Total Carb **1g** • Fiber **0g** • Total Sugars **0g** • Protein **10g**

Brown Rice Dolmas

These lemony parcels of herbed brown rice are simple to make and surprisingly tasty. The flavors of dill, mint, garlic, onion, and lemon are all packaged up in grape leaves to make a fun and unique appetizer or snack.

PROGRAM
Pressure Cook (High)

RELEASE
Natural and Quick

Gluten-Free, Dairy-Free, Vegan

Makes **12 dolmas**   Serving Size **6 dolmas**   Prep Time **20 mins**   Pressure Time **12 mins**   Total Time **55 mins**

1 cup Fluffy Brown Rice (page 95), cooled

2 tbsp olive oil, divided

2 tsp lemon juice, divided

1 tsp finely chopped dill

1 tsp finely chopped mint leaves

½ tsp onion powder

¼ tsp garlic powder

¼ tsp salt

¼ tsp black pepper

12 jarred grape leaves

1 cup water

1. In a medium bowl, stir together the rice, 1 tablespoon olive oil, 1 teaspoon lemon juice, dill, mint, onion powder, garlic powder, salt, and pepper.

2. Working one at a time, lay the grape leaves flat, shiny-side down on your workspace. Place ¹⁄₁₂ of the rice mixture (about 1 heaping tablespoon) at the base of each leaf. Start rolling up from the bottom, folding in the sides as you go. Roll all the way up to the tip of the leaf to make 2- to 3-inch (5–7.5cm) long rolls. Continue until you have rolled all 12 dolmas.

3. Place the dolmas in a single layer in a 6-inch (15.25cm) round stainless steel pan or glass baking dish. Pour 1 cup water and the remaining 1 tablespoon olive oil and 1 teaspoon lemon juice over the dolmas. Place another smaller glass bowl, baking dish, or oven-safe plate on top of the dolmas to weigh them down so they don't unroll while cooking.

4. Place the steam rack in the inner pot and add 1 cup water. Place the pan of weighed-down dolmas onto the steam rack. Lock the lid and set the steam release valve to the sealing position. Select **Pressure Cook (High),** and set the cook time for **12 minutes.**

5. Once the cook time is complete, allow the pressure to release naturally for 5 minutes, then quick release any remaining pressure. Using tongs, carefully remove the dolmas to a serving tray. Discard the remaining liquid. Serve warm or chilled.

TIP | This recipe is a great way to use up rice left over from another meal. You can easily use white rice instead of brown rice.

Jarred grape leaves are usually found in the international foods or canned vegetable section of the grocery store.

NUTRITION PER SERVING:
Calories **241** • Total Fat **14.7g** • Total Carb **26g** • Fiber **4g** • Total Sugars **1g** • Protein **4g**

Meat Lovers Crustless Mini Quiche Bites

PROGRAM
**Sauté (More),
Pressure Cook (High)**

RELEASE
Natural and Quick

**Gluten-Free,
Keto Friendly**

These little quiche bites are packed with protein and make a great midafternoon snack or a cute addition to any brunch. Even though they're very low in carbs, these baby quiche are still bursting with flavor.

Makes **4 quiche bites**   Serving Size **2 quiche bites**   Prep Time **15 mins**   Pressure Time **12 mins**   Total Time **45 mins**

2 slices uncooked bacon, chopped

¼ cup finely diced ham

¼ cup finely diced yellow onion

3 large eggs

2 tbsp sour cream

¼ cup shredded Cheddar cheese

¼ tsp black pepper

Chopped chives (optional), for garnish

1. Select **Sauté (More).** Once the pot is hot, add the bacon and sauté for 3 minutes. Add the ham and onion, and sauté for 3 minutes more. Press **Cancel** and remove the mixture from the inner pot with a slotted spoon, discarding any excess bacon fat. Set aside to cool slightly.

2. In a small bowl, whisk together the eggs, sour cream, Cheddar, and pepper, and stir in the meat mixture.

3. Spray 4 (4fl oz; 120ml) canning jars with nonstick spray, and divide the egg mixture between them. Place the steam rack in the inner pot and add 1 cup water. Place the jars on the steam rack.

4. Lock the lid and set the steam release valve to the sealing position. Select **Pressure Cook (High),** and set the cook time for **12 minutes.**

5. Once the cook time is complete, allow the pressure to release naturally for 5 minutes, then quick release any remaining pressure.

6. Allow the quiche to cool in the jars on a wire rack for 5 minutes. Run a butter knife around the inside edges of the jars to make them easier to remove, if desired. Top with chopped chives, if desired, and serve immediately.

TIP These quiche bites reheat well. Prep a batch ahead of time and keep them in an airtight container in the refrigerator to pull out when a snack craving hits.

This recipe is a great way to use up leftovers. Substitute the diced ham with leftover ground beef crumbles, breakfast sausage, or even grilled chicken.

NUTRITION PER SERVING:
Calories **338** • Total Fat **26.2g** • Total Carb **2g** • Fiber **0g** • Total Sugars **1g** • Protein **23g**

Sweet Chili Chicken Meatballs

These meatballs are drenched with a delicious, from-scratch sweet chili sauce that is surprisingly easy to throw together and completely avoids the white sugar and high-fructose corn syrup typically found in store-bought sauces.

PROGRAM
**Pressure Cook (High),
Sauté (More)**

RELEASE
Natural and Quick

**Gluten-Free,
Dairy-Free**

Serves **2**   Serving Size **5 meatballs**   Prep Time **10 mins**   Pressure Time **5 mins**   Total Time **30 mins**

Chopped cilantro, for garnish

For the meatballs:
6oz (170g) ground chicken
1 tbsp finely chopped scallions
1 egg yolk
1 tbsp blanched almond flour
1 tbsp cassava flour
¼ tsp salt
¼ tsp black pepper
1 tsp avocado oil or olive oil

For the sweet chili sauce:
¼ cup water
2 tbsp coconut sugar
1 tbsp rice vinegar
1 tsp fish sauce
Dash of garlic powder
½ tsp red pepper flakes
¼ tsp salt
1 tsp arrowroot starch

1. Prepare the meatballs. In a small bowl, combine the ground chicken, scallions, egg yolk, almond flour, cassava flour, salt, and pepper. (This is easiest when done by hand.) Form into 10 (1in; 2.5cm) meatballs.

2. Place a steamer basket with feet and 1 cup water in the inner pot. Spray the bottom of the steamer basket with nonstick spray. Place the meatballs in the steamer basket in a single layer. Lock the lid and set the steam release valve to the sealing position. Select **Pressure Cook (High),** and set the cook time for **5 minutes.**

3. While the meatballs are cooking, prepare the sweet chili sauce. In a small bowl, whisk together ¼ cup water, coconut sugar, rice vinegar, fish sauce, garlic powder, red pepper flakes, salt, and starch. Set aside.

4. Once the cook time is complete, allow the pressure to release naturally for 5 minutes, then quick release any remaining pressure. Press **Cancel** to turn off Keep Warm. Remove the steamer basket and set aside. Discard the water and replace the inner pot.

5. Select **Sauté (More)** and add the oil. Once the pot is hot, add the steamed meatballs and allow to cook undisturbed for 4 minutes on each side.

6. Pour the sweet chili sauce into the inner pot. Bring up to a boil, stirring constantly until thickened and bubbly, about 1 minute. Transfer the meatballs to a serving dish and garnish with chopped cilantro. Serve immediately.

TIP | The sweet chili sauce is a delicious condiment that enhances many other dishes, such as dumplings, chicken tenders, and fried rice. Whip up the sauce mixture anytime, and simmer for 2 minutes until thickened. Transfer to a jar and store covered in the refrigerator for up to 1 month.

NUTRITION PER SERVING:
Calories **214** • Total Fat **9.9g** • Total Carb **16g** • Fiber **1g** • Total Sugars **10g** • Protein **17g**

Steamed Pork and Ginger Dumplings

These steamed dumplings are a delicious treat fresh out of your Instant Pot. With all of the flavors packed into these little bundles, you won't even miss the fried versions at your local Chinese restaurant!

PROGRAM
Pressure Cook (High)

RELEASE
Quick

Dairy-Free

Makes **6 dumplings**   Serving Size **3 dumplings**   Prep Time **20 mins**   Pressure Time **4 mins**   Total Time **35 mins**

3oz (85g) ground pork

1½ tsp tamari

½ tsp toasted sesame oil

1 tsp minced fresh ginger

⅛ tsp onion powder

⅛ tsp salt

6 premade square wonton or dumpling wrappers, about 3½ sq in (9 sq cm) each (usually found in refrigerated section)

¼ cup Asian Plum Sauce (page 51; optional)

1. In a medium bowl, mix together the ground pork, tamari, sesame oil, ginger, onion powder, and salt. (This is easiest when done by hand.)

   Fill a small dish with water. Working one at a time, lay a wonton wrapper flat on your workspace. Place ⅙ of the pork mixture in the center. Dip your finger into the water and run it along the four edges of the wrapper to dampen. Pick up two opposite corners of the wrapper and bring them together over the filling, pressing together so that they stick. Pick up the other two corners of the wrapper and bring them up so that all four corners meet together in the middle. Press out as much air as possible, and seal up the edges by pinching them together. The top of the dumpling will look like an X. Dip your thumb and forefinger into the dish of water and grab one corner of the X. Fold it in so that it sticks to the side of the dumpling. Repeat with the other 3 corners, folding them all in the same direction to make a swirl.

2. Place a steamer basket with feet in the inner pot and add 1 cup water. Spray the bottom of the basket with nonstick spray, and arrange the dumplings in a single layer.

3. Lock the lid and set the steam release valve to the sealing position. Select **Pressure Cook (High),** and set the cook time for **4 minutes.**

4. Once the cook time is complete, quick release the pressure. With tongs, carefully remove the dumplings to a serving tray. Serve immediately along with Asian Plum Sauce for dipping, if desired.

TIP | If pork is not your thing, try this recipe with ground chicken instead.

NUTRITION PER SERVING (EXCLUDING ASIAN PLUM SAUCE):
Calories **216** • Total Fat **12.8g** • Total Carb **14g** • Fiber **1g** • Total Sugars **0g** • Protein **10g**

Mu Shu Vegetable Dumplings

These tasty vegetarian dumplings make a wonderfully light appetizer. They are steamed to perfection with a savory egg and vegetable filling and pair perfectly with the sweet Asian Plum Sauce for dipping.

PROGRAM
Pressure Cook (High)

RELEASE
Quick

Gluten-Free

Makes **6 dumplings**   Serving Size **3 dumplings**   Prep Time **20 mins**   Pressure Time **4 mins**   Total Time **35 mins**

2 tbsp shredded and finely chopped cabbage

2 tbsp very finely chopped shiitake mushrooms (or cremini mushrooms)

2 tbsp shredded carrot

1 medium scallion, sliced in half lengthwise and very finely chopped

1 large egg white

1 tsp tamari

¼ tsp toasted sesame oil

¼ tsp ginger powder

6 premade square wonton or dumpling wrappers, about 3½ sq in (9 sq cm) each (usually found in refrigerated section)

¼ cup Asian Plum Sauce (page 51), or use store-bought plum sauce

1. In a medium bowl, mix together the cabbage, mushrooms, carrot, scallion, egg white, tamari, sesame oil, and ginger.

Fill a small dish with water. Working one at a time, lay a wonton wrapper flat on your workspace. Place ⅙ of the egg and vegetable mixture in the center of the wrapper. Dip your finger into the water and run it along the four edges of the wrapper to dampen. Pick up two opposite corners of the wrapper and bring them together over the filling. Press them together so they stick. Pick up the other two corners of the wrapper and bring them up so that all four corners meet together in the middle. Press out as much air as possible, and seal up the edges by pinching them together. The top of the dumpling will look like an *X*. Dip your thumb and forefinger into the dish of water and grab one corner of the *X*. Fold it in so that it sticks to the side of the dumpling. Repeat with the other 3 corners, folding them all in the same direction to make a swirl.

2. Place a steamer basket with feet in the inner pot and add 1 cup water. Spray the bottom of the basket with nonstick spray, and arrange the dumplings in a single layer.

3. Lock the lid and set the steam release valve to the sealing position. Select **Pressure Cook (High),** and set the cook time for **4 minutes.**

4. Once the cook time is complete, quick release the pressure. With tongs, carefully remove the dumplings to a serving tray. Serve immediately along with Asian Plum Sauce for dipping.

TIP | Easily double this recipe. Use 1 whole egg if doubling, and cook the dumplings in 2 batches to avoid them sticking together.

NUTRITION PER SERVING (EXCLUDING ASIAN PLUM SAUCE):
Calories **100** • Total Fat **1.1g** • Total Carb **17g** • Fiber **1g** • Total Sugars **1g** • Protein **6g**

Mexican Stuffed Mini Peppers

PROGRAM
Pressure Cook (High)

RELEASE
Quick

**Gluten-Free,
Keto Friendly**

These cute little stuffed peppers are a great snack or a perfect way to start off your meal. Bursting with flavor, very low in carbs, and providing a healthy serving of veggies, you really can't go wrong with this appetizer!

Makes **8 peppers**   Serving Size **4 peppers**   Prep Time **15 mins**   Pressure Time **2 mins**   Total Time **30 mins**

3oz (85g) lean ground beef

1 tbsp blanched almond flour

½ tsp chili powder

¼ tsp dried oregano

¼ tsp ground cumin

⅛ tsp garlic powder

⅛ tsp onion powder

½ tsp salt

⅛ tsp black pepper

2 tbsp shredded Cheddar cheese

8 mini sweet bell peppers

For the dipping sauce:

2 tbsp sour cream

¼ tsp chili powder

2 tsp lime juice

⅛ tsp salt

1 tbsp finely chopped scallions, for garnish

1 tbsp finely chopped cilantro, for garnish

1. In a small bowl, mix together the ground beef, almond flour, chili powder, oregano, cumin, garlic powder, onion powder, salt, pepper, and Cheddar.

2. Slice the tops off the bell peppers, and scoop out the seeds. Stuff each pepper with an equal amount of the ground beef filling, pressing it down firmly.

3. Place a steamer basket with feet in the inner pot and add 1 cup water. Add the peppers to the steamer basket. Lock the lid and set the steam release valve to the sealing position. Select **Pressure Cook (High),** and set the cook time for **2 minutes.**

4. While the peppers are cooking, make the dipping sauce. In a small serving bowl, stir together the sour cream, chili powder, lime juice, and salt. Refrigerate until ready to serve.

5. Once the cook time is complete, quick release the pressure. Arrange the peppers on a serving dish along with the dipping sauce. Sprinkle the scallions and cilantro over the dipping sauce, and serve immediately.

TIP | Try this recipe with ground chicken instead of ground beef.

NUTRITION PER SERVING:
Calories **227** • Total Fat **12.4g** • Total Carb **15g** • Fiber **3g** • Total Sugars **1g** • Protein **16g**

Mini–Mason Jar Corn Dog Muffins

PROGRAM
Pressure Cook (High)

RELEASE
Natural and Quick

Gluten-Free

Bring out your inner little kid with these fun corn dog muffins right from your Instant Pot. The taste will bring you back to being at a country fair, just without any of the gluten or a deep fryer!

Makes **4 mini muffins** Serving Size **2 mini muffins** Prep Time **10 mins** Pressure Time **11 min** Total Time **45 mins**

1 tbsp salted butter, melted and slightly cooled

2 tbsp buttermilk

1 tbsp honey

1 large egg white

2 tbsp (16g) cassava flour

2 tbsp (22g) medium grind yellow or white cornmeal

¼ tsp baking soda

⅛ tsp salt

1 beef hot dog, about 2oz (55g), cut into ¼-in (0.5cm) rounds

Ketchup and mustard (optional), for serving

1. In a small bowl, whisk together the butter, buttermilk, honey, and egg white. In a separate medium bowl, stir together the cassava flour, cornmeal, baking soda, and salt.

2. Gently stir the buttermilk mixture into the flour mixture, just until combined. Fold in the hot dog rounds.

3. Spray 4 (4fl oz; 120ml) canning jars with nonstick spray, and gently divide the batter between them.

4. Place the steam rack in the inner pot and add 1 cup water. Place the jars on the steam rack and rest the flat canning lid on top of each to keep out excess moisture. (There is no need to screw on the ring.)

5. Lock the lid and set the steam release valve to the sealing position. Select **Pressure Cook (High),** and set the cook time for **11 minutes.**

6. Once the cook time is complete, allow the pressure to release naturally for 5 minutes, then quick release any remaining pressure.

7. Allow the muffins to cool in the jars, uncovered, on a wire rack for 5 minutes. Run a butter knife around the inside edges of the jars to make them easier to remove from the jars, if desired. Serve immediately with ketchup and mustard for dipping, if desired. Store with the lids screwed on in the refrigerator for up to 3 days.

TIP | These muffins store well and are a fun addition to any sack lunch. Just reheat in the microwave for a few seconds and enjoy.

NUTRITION PER SERVING:
Calories **231** • Total Fat **13.2g** • Total Carb **23g** • Fiber **1g** • Total Sugars **10g** • Protein **6g**

Renae's Favorite Hummus

Hummus is the perfect addition to so many things. Just ask four-year-old Renae! She loves it as a dip for veggies (especially snap peas) and crackers, or as a spread on sandwiches or lettuce wraps.

PROGRAM
Bean/Chili (High)

RELEASE
Natural and Quick

Gluten-Free, Dairy-Free, Vegan

Makes **about 1 cup**   Serving Size **2 tablespoons**   Prep Time **5 mins**   Pressure Time **40 mins**   Total Time **1 hour 30 mins**

3oz (85g) dried chickpeas, rinsed (about ½ cup)

2 cups water

1 tbsp plus 2 tsp olive oil, divided

2 tbsp tahini

1 clove garlic, roughly chopped

1 tsp salt

⅛ tsp black pepper

1 tbsp fresh lemon juice

½ tsp za'atar seasoning (optional)

Smoked paprika, for garnish

Chopped parsley, for garnish

1. Add the chickpeas, 2 cups water, and 1 teaspoon olive oil to the inner pot. Lock the lid and set the steam release valve to the sealing position. Select **Bean/Chili (High),** and set the cook time for **40 minutes.**

2. Once the cook time is complete, allow the pressure to release naturally for 10 minutes, then quick release any remaining pressure.

3. Using a fine-mesh strainer, drain the chickpeas, reserving the cooking liquid. Allow the beans to cool for 5 minutes, then transfer to a blender or food processor.

4. Along with the beans, add 1 tablespoon olive oil, tahini, garlic, salt, pepper, lemon juice, za'atar seasoning (if using), and ¼ cup reserved cooking liquid. Blend until smooth, stopping to scrape down the sides of the blender periodically, if needed.

5. Transfer the hummus to a serving dish and drizzle with the remaining 1 teaspoon olive oil. Sprinkle with paprika and chopped parsley, and serve immediately. Keep leftover hummus in an airtight container in the refrigerator for up to 5 days.

TIP Za'atar is a delicious seasoning blend that includes sesame, sumac, and other spices. You can often find it in Middle Eastern grocery stores or health food stores in the spices section. It adds delicious flavor to this hummus recipe but can be omitted if desired.

To make a za'atar spice blend at home, combine 1 teaspoon each dried thyme leaves, dried oregano leaves, and hulled sesame seeds; ½ teaspoon salt; and 1½ teaspoons sumac powder. Use a mortar and pestle to crush the spice mixture together, and store in an airtight container until use.

NUTRITION PER SERVING:

Calories **66** • Total Fat **3.5g** • Total Carb **7g** • Fiber **1g** • Total Sugars **1g** • Protein **2g**

Bacon and Bleu Cheese–Stuffed Mushroom Caps

PROGRAM
**Sauté (More),
Pressure Cook (High)**

RELEASE
Quick

**Gluten-Free,
Keto Friendly**

What better way to start your meal than bacon, bleu cheese, and an extra serving of veggies at nearly zero carbs? White mushroom caps become the perfect delivery system for this creamy bleu cheese filling and crispy bacon.

Serves **2**   Serving Size **4 mushrooms**   Prep Time **15 mins**   Pressure Time **1 min**   Total Time **25 mins**

2 slices uncooked bacon, chopped

2 tbsp cream cheese, room temperature

1 tbsp bleu cheese crumbles

1 tbsp blanched almond flour

½ tsp Worcestershire sauce (gluten-free, if needed)

8 small white mushrooms, about 1½in (3.75cm) in diameter

Chopped parsley, for garnish

1. Select **Sauté (More).** Once the pot is hot, add the bacon. Sauté until browned and crispy. Remove the bacon with a slotted spoon and place on a paper towel–lined plate to drain, leaving behind the rendered bacon fat. Press **Cancel** to turn off Sauté. Reserve half of the bacon crumbles for garnish. Finely chop the remaining bacon.

2. In a small bowl, mix together the finely chopped bacon, cream cheese, bleu cheese, almond flour, and Worcestershire sauce. Wash the mushrooms and carefully pop out the stems, leaving only the mushroom caps. Fill each cap with about 1 teaspoon cream cheese mixture.

3. Arrange the mushroom caps in a single layer around the perimeter of the inner pot, and add 2 tablespoons water to the bottom of the pot. Lock the lid and set the steam release valve to the sealing position. Select **Pressure Cook (High),** and set the cook time for **1 minute.**

4. Once the cook time is complete, quick release the pressure. Carefully transfer the mushrooms to a paper towel-lined plate to soak up any excess moisture. Transfer to a serving platter, sprinkle with the reserved bacon crumbles and parsley, and serve immediately.

TIP | Mushrooms naturally contain a lot of liquid that gets released quickly when cooking. Recipes with mushrooms require only a little bit of extra water—2 tablespoons—in order for the Instant Pot to come up to pressure.

NUTRITION PER SERVING:
Calories **180** • Total Fat **15.8g** • Total Carb **3g** • Fiber **1g** • Total Sugars **2g** • Protein **7g**

Cheesy Taco Dip

This zesty dip is packed with protein and is sure to please. It is delicious served with tortilla chips, but you can keep the appetizer low in carbs by serving along with a raw veggie tray or your favorite low-carb crackers.

PROGRAM
**Sauté (More),
Pressure Cook (High)**

RELEASE
Natural and Quick

**Gluten-Free,
Keto Friendly**

Serves **4**   Serving Size **about ½ cup**   Prep Time **15 mins**   Pressure Time **4 mins**   Total Time **35 mins**

1 tsp avocado oil or olive oil

¼ cup finely chopped yellow onion

6oz (170g) lean ground beef

½ cup beef broth or water

2oz (55g) canned fire-roasted diced green chiles

½ cup finely diced tomatoes, divided

1 tsp chili powder

¼ tsp dried oregano

⅛ tsp garlic powder

½ tsp salt

¼ tsp black pepper

¼ cup half & half

2 tsp arrowroot starch, or cornstarch

2 tbsp cream cheese

½ cup shredded Cheddar cheese

Chopped cilantro, for garnish

1. Select **Sauté (More),** and add the oil to the inner pot. When hot, add the onion and sauté for 2 minutes. Add the ground beef and sauté for 4 minutes more, breaking it up into very small crumbles.

2. Press **Cancel** and drain away any excess rendered fat from the meat. Stir in the broth or water, green chiles, ¼ cup diced tomatoes, chili powder, oregano, garlic powder, salt, and pepper.

3. Lock the lid and set the steam release valve to the sealing position. Select **Pressure Cook (High),** and set the cook time for **4 minutes.**

4. Once the cook time is complete, allow the pressure to release naturally for 5 minutes, then quick release any remaining pressure.

5. Press **Cancel** and select **Sauté (More).** In a small bowl, whisk together the half & half and starch. Stir the mixture into the inner pot. Bring just up to a simmer, then remove the inner pot from the base.

6. Stir in the cream cheese and Cheddar until both are melted and smooth. Transfer the dip to a serving bowl and top with the remaining ¼ cup diced tomatoes and chopped cilantro. Serve warm.

TIP | This recipe also works well with ground chicken or ground turkey.

NUTRITION PER SERVING:
Calories **242** • Total Fat **18.7g** • Total Carb **6g** • Fiber **1g** • Total Sugars **3g** • Protein **12g**

Basil and Greek Olive White Bean Dip

PROGRAM
Bean/Chili (High)

RELEASE
Natural and Quick

Gluten-Free, Dairy-Free, Keto Friendly, Vegan

This savory dip is filled with fiber and protein from the white beans and pairs well with crisp veggies, pita bread, or crackers. The salty punch of flavor from the olives and the bright fresh basil make it easy to just keep dipping!

Makes **1½ cups**   Serving Size **2 tbsp**   Prep Time **5 mins**   Pressure Time **35 mins**   Total Time **1 hour 10 mins**

3oz (85g) dried Great Northern beans, rinsed

2 cups water

2 tbsp plus 1 tsp olive oil, divided

1 tsp lemon juice

¼ tsp garlic powder

¼ tsp red pepper flakes

½ tsp salt

¼ tsp black pepper

¼ cup chopped basil (loosely packed)

¼ cup roughly chopped kalamata olives

1. Add the beans, 2 cups water, and 1 teaspoon olive oil to the inner pot. Lock the lid and set the steam release valve to the sealing position. Select **Bean/Chili (High),** and set the cook time for **35 minutes.**

2. Once the cook time is complete, allow the pressure to release naturally for 10 minutes, then quick release any remaining pressure.

3. Using a fine-mesh strainer, drain the beans, reserving the liquid. Allow the beans to cool for 5 minutes, and then transfer to a blender or food processor.

4. Along with the beans, add the remaining 2 tablespoons olive oil, lemon juice, garlic powder, red pepper flakes, salt, and pepper. Blend until smooth, adding 2 to 4 tablespoons reserved cooking liquid if necessary to reach the desired consistency.

5. Add the basil and olives, and pulse the blender until they are very finely minced but not fully puréed. Transfer the dip to a serving dish and serve immediately. Keep leftover dip in an airtight container in the refrigerator for up to 5 days.

NUTRITION PER SERVING:
Calories **42** • Total Fat **3.6g** • Total Carb **2g** • Fiber **1g** • Total Sugars **0g** • Protein **1g**

Creamy Pesto Chicken Dip

This warm chicken dip served with crisp veggies makes a scrumptious appetizer that is also very low in carbs. Rich, creamy cheeses and vivid green basil bring the perfect flavors and textures to this comfort food recipe.

PROGRAM
Pressure Cook (High)

RELEASE
Natural and Quick

**Gluten-Free,
Keto Friendly**

Serves **4**   Serving Size **about ⅓ cup dip**   Prep Time **5 mins**   Pressure Time **11 mins**   Total Time **35 mins**

6oz (170g) chicken thigh meat, cubed

¼ cup Chicken Bone Broth (page 44) or store-bought chicken broth

4oz (110g) ⅓-less-fat cream cheese

3 tbsp sour cream

4 tbsp shredded Parmesan cheese, divided

1 cup basil leaves (loosely packed)

1 tbsp roasted pine nuts or walnuts

1 clove garlic

2 tsp olive oil

¼ tsp salt

¼ tsp black pepper

Raw vegetables, for serving

1. Add the chicken and broth to the inner pot. Lock the lid and set the steam release valve to the sealing position. Select **Pressure Cook (High),** and set the cook time for **3 minutes.**

2. While the chicken cooks, in the bowl of a food processer or blender, add the cream cheese, sour cream, 2 tablespoons Parmesan, basil, pine nuts, garlic, olive oil, salt, and pepper. Blend until smooth. Transfer the mixture to a small oven-safe bowl or baking dish that is able to fit into the inner pot.

3. Once the cook time is complete, allow the pressure to release naturally for 5 minutes, then quick release any remaining pressure. Press **Cancel** to turn off Keep Warm.

4. Remove the chicken from the inner pot, leaving the liquid in the bottom. Finely chop the cooked chicken and stir into the basil–cream cheese mixture. Smooth out the top of the mixture in the baking dish, and sprinkle with the remaining 2 tablespoons Parmesan. Cover with a lid or aluminum foil.

5. Place the steam rack in the inner pot and add additional water, if needed, so you have 1 cup liquid. Place the baking dish on the steam rack. Lock the lid and set the steam release valve to the sealing position. Select **Pressure Cook (High),** and set the cook time for **8 minutes.**

6. Once the cook time is complete, quick release the pressure. Serve immediately with the raw vegetables.

TIP | Take a shortcut by using 3 tablespoons premade basil pesto in place of the basil, pine nuts, garlic, and olive oil.

This recipe is a great way to use up leftover chicken from a previous meal. Skip the chicken thigh and Step 1, and substitute with ¾ cup finely chopped cooked chicken.

NUTRITION PER SERVING (EXCLUDING VEGETABLES FOR SERVING):
Calories **188** • Total Fat **13.3g** • Total Carb **3g** • Fiber **0g** • Total Sugars **1g** • Protein **14g**

Desserts

Drunken Apples
with Whiskey and Raisins

This light and fun dessert has a melody of unique flavors. The bite of the ginger, cardamom, and whiskey is offset by the sweetness of the apple and raisins and complemented by the zing of the orange zest.

PROGRAM
Pressure Cook (High)

RELEASE
Quick

Gluten-Free, Dairy-Free, Vegan

Serves **2**   Serving Size **½ apple**   Prep Time **15 mins**   Pressure Time **5 mins**   Total Time **35 mins**

1 crisp, medium Gala apple (or other sweet variety, such as Fuji, Braeburn, Jonagold, or Cameo)

2 tsp coconut oil, melted

2 tbsp old-fashioned rolled oats (certified gluten-free, if needed)

1 tbsp cassava flour

1 tbsp raisins

2 tsp coconut sugar

Pinch of ground cardamom

Pinch of ginger powder

Pinch of salt

1½ tsp bourbon

Zest of ½ small orange

Drizzle of coconut milk (optional), for serving

1. Cut the apple in half. Cut or scoop out the seeds and enough of the flesh to make a 2-inch (5cm) well in each. In a small bowl, mix together the coconut oil, rolled oats, cassava flour, raisins, coconut sugar, cardamom, ginger, salt, and bourbon.

2. Scoop the filling evenly into the wells of each apple half. Sprinkle the apples with the orange zest.

3. Place the steam rack in the inner pot and add 1 cup water. Place the apples on the steam rack. Lock the lid and set the steam release valve to the sealing position. Select **Pressure Cook (High),** and set the cook time for **5 minutes.**

4. Once the cook time is complete, quick release the pressure. With tongs, carefully remove the apples to a serving dish and drizzle with the coconut milk, if desired. Serve immediately.

TIP | If you like a softer cooked apple, increase the cook time by 1 minute. If you prefer your apple on the firmer side, decrease the cook time by 1 minute.

Prep the apples ahead of time through Step 2, and refrigerate until you're ready to cook them. Before storing, just moisten the exposed part of the apple with a bit of lemon juice to prevent browning. Throw the prepared apples in the Instant Pot at a moment's notice, and this fragrant dessert is ready to go in a matter of minutes.

For a nutty variation, add a tablespoon of finely chopped walnuts or pecans.

NUTRITION PER SERVING (EXCLUDING COCONUT MILK):
Calories **163** • Total Fat **4.9g** • Total Carb **28g** • Fiber **3g** • Total Sugars **14g** • Protein **1g**

Honey-Vanilla Peach Topping

PROGRAM
**Pressure Cook (High),
Sauté (Normal)**

RELEASE
Natural and Quick

**Gluten-Free, Dairy-
Free, Vegan**

This versatile recipe can enhance so many dishes, as well as make your house smell amazing! Try it poured over ice cream or Greek yogurt, or use it to top waffles, pancakes, or even cheesecake. The Instant Pot does such a good job at breaking down fruit that peeling the peaches isn't even necessary.

Serves **2**   Serving Size **½ cup**   Prep Time **5 mins**   Pressure Time **1 min**   Total Time **35 mins**

8oz (225g) diced peaches (about 1 large or 2 small)

2 tsp coconut oil

½ tsp pure vanilla extract

3 tbsp water, divided

3 tbsp honey

1 tsp arrowroot starch, or cornstarch

1. To the inner pot, add the peaches, coconut oil, vanilla, and 2 tablespoons water, and stir to combine. Drizzle the honey on top of the peach mixture, but do not stir.

2. Lock the lid and set the steam release valve to the sealing position. Select **Pressure Cook (High),** and set the cook time for **1 minute.**

3. In a small bowl, whisk together the starch and the remaining 1 tablespoon water. Set aside.

4. Once the cook time is complete, allow the pressure to release naturally for 5 minutes, then quick release any remaining pressure. Press **Cancel** to turn off Keep Warm.

5. Select **Sauté (Normal),** and bring the pot up to a simmer. Stir in the starch and water mixture, and allow to simmer until the liquid is thickened, about 1 minute. Remove the inner pot from the base and let cool for 10 minutes before serving. Store any leftovers in an airtight container in the refrigerator for up to 5 days.

TIP | For a variation, try this recipe with apples or pears.

Honey and other sugars tend to scorch on the bottom of the Instant Pot. We avoid this by drizzling the honey on top of the peaches without stirring it in.

NUTRITION PER SERVING:
Calories **189** • Total Fat **4.7g** • Total Carb **38g** • Fiber **2g** • Total Sugars **36g** • Protein **1g**

Chocolate Fondue Dip

This versatile chocolate dip is sure to be a crowd pleaser. Turn your Instant Pot into a fondue warmer and serve with any number of dippables, such as strawberries, banana slices, marshmallows, gluten-free graham crackers, or pretzels.

PROGRAM
**Sauté (More),
Keep Warm**

RELEASE
None

Gluten-Free

Makes **1 cup**　　Serving Size **¼ cup**　　Prep Time **5 mins**　　Pressure Time **None**　　Total Time **15 mins**

1 cup semisweet chocolate chips

½ cup half & half

¼ tsp pure vanilla extract

1. Add 2 cups water to the inner pot and select **Sauté (More).** Create a double boiler by placing a stainless steel or glass bowl with a rounded bottom and a diameter of at least 9 inches (23cm) on top of the inner pot.

2. To the bowl, add the chocolate chips, half & half, and vanilla. Allow the chocolate mixture to heat up, stirring often, until it is melted and smooth. This will take 5 to 10 minutes. (The bowl will get very hot, so always use hot pads to secure it while stirring.)

3. Once the chocolate is smooth, press **Cancel** and select **Keep Warm.** This will keep your fondue at a perfect dipping consistency.

4. Either keep the bowl on the Instant Pot while serving to keep it warm (like with a fondue pot), or transfer the bowl to a heat-resistant surface and serve with your choice of items to dip. If the chocolate in the bowl begins to cool and harden, place the bowl over the water in the inner pot again, selecting **Sauté (more),** and heat and stir until you again reach the desired consistency.

TIP　Try fun variations of this fondue by using milk chocolate or white chocolate chips instead of semisweet.

This dip also doubles as a delicious hot fudge sauce. Try it on an ice cream sundae!

You can easily double all of the ingredients to serve a crowd!

NUTRITION PER SERVING:
Calories **286** • Total Fat **16.4g** • Total Carb **36g** • Fiber **4g** • Total Sugars **32g** • Protein **4g**

Sticky Coconut Rice with Mango

PROGRAM
Pressure Cook (Low)

RELEASE
Quick

**Gluten-Free,
Dairy-Free, Vegan**

This variation of a classic Thai dessert comes with a fraction of the sugar and labor of the original, but it is equally as satisfying and refreshing. You'll love the fragrant coconut rice, perfectly complemented by the bite of juicy mango.

Serves **2**   Serving Size **½ cup rice plus ½ mango**   Prep Time **5 mins**   Pressure Time **20 mins**   Total Time **40 mins**

½ cup sticky rice (also called *glutinous* or *sweet rice*)

½ cup water

¼ cup full-fat coconut milk

1 tbsp coconut sugar

1 small, fresh mango, peeled and sliced, or 1 cup frozen mango, thawed

Sprinkle of black sesame seeds, for garnish

Sprinkle of lime zest, for garnish

1. Place the steam rack in the inner pot and add 1 cup water. To a 6-inch (15.25cm) round stainless steel pan that fits in the inner pot, add the sticky rice and ½ cup water. Place the pan, uncovered, on the steam rack in the inner pot.

2. Lock the lid and set the steam release valve to the sealing position. Select **Pressure Cook (Low),** and set the cook time for **20 minutes.**

3. While the rice is cooking, in a small bowl, whisk together the coconut milk and coconut sugar. Peel and slice the mango.

4. Once the cook time is complete, quick release the pressure. Remove the pan from the inner pot. Add the coconut milk mixture to the rice, and fluff with a fork to combine. Let the rice rest for 5 minutes to soak up the coconut milk.

5. Portion the sticky rice onto two serving bowls or plates, and arrange half of the sliced mango with each. Garnish with black sesame seeds and lime zest, and serve immediately.

TIP Despite its name, glutinous rice is actually gluten-free. You can find it in most Asian grocery stores or online.

NUTRITION PER SERVING:
Calories **262** • Total Fat **6.7g** • Total Carb **51g** • Fiber **3g** • Total Sugars **27g** • Protein **3g**

Christmas Eve
Cinnamon Rice Pudding

PROGRAM
**Pressure Cook (High),
Sauté (Less)**

RELEASE
Natural and Quick

**Gluten-Free, Dairy-
Free Variation**

Spiced up with cinnamon and vanilla, this sweet and warming rice pudding makes for a wonderful light dessert or a perfect evening treat to enjoy while wrapping presents or waiting for Santa Claus to arrive!

Serves **2**   Serving Size **1 cup**   Prep Time **5 mins**   Pressure Time **8 mins**   Total Time **30 mins**

½ cup short-grain white pearl rice, rinsed

¾ cup water

¼ tsp salt

1 cup whole milk

3 tbsp coconut sugar

½ tsp ground cinnamon, plus more for serving

1 tsp pure vanilla extract

2 tsp arrowroot starch, or cornstarch

1. Add the rice, ¾ cup water, and salt to the inner pot, and stir to combine. Lock the lid and set the steam release valve to the sealing position. Select **Pressure Cook (High),** and set the cook time for **8 minutes.**

2. While the rice is cooking, to a small bowl, add the milk, coconut sugar, cinnamon, vanilla, and starch. Whisk to combine.

3. Once the cook time is complete, allow the pressure to release naturally for 5 minutes, then quickly release any remaining pressure. Press **Cancel.**

4. Select **Sauté (Less),** and stir the milk mixture into the rice. Bring to a simmer and allow to cook, stirring constantly, for 1 minute until the milk begins to thicken. Immediately remove the inner pot from the base. Portion the rice pudding into two serving bowls. Sprinkle each with a bit of cinnamon, and serve immediately.

TIP | Make it dairy-free: Substitute light coconut milk for the whole milk.

NUTRITION PER SERVING:
Calories **316** • Total Fat **4.3g** • Total Carb **62g** • Fiber **0g** • Total Sugars **20g** • Protein **7g**

Lemon Olive Oil Polenta Cake

This fragrant cake is lightly sweetened with honey, and the polenta gives it a unique and delicious texture. It's a take on a classic Italian dessert and makes a great addition to a brunch or an afternoon cup of tea.

PROGRAM
Pressure Cook (High)

RELEASE
Natural and Quick

Gluten-Free, Dairy-Free

Serves **6**   Serving Size **⅙ cake**   Prep Time **15 mins**   Pressure Time **35 mins**   Total Time **1 hour 25 mins**

⅓ cup (37g) blanched almond flour

⅓ cup (46g) dry polenta (also called *corn grits*, not quick grits)

1 tsp baking soda

¼ tsp salt

3 tbsp plus ½ tsp extra-virgin olive oil, divided

1 tbsp fresh lemon juice

Zest of 1 lemon

1 large egg, lightly beaten

¼ cup honey

1 tsp pure vanilla extract

Powdered sugar, for dusting

1. In a medium bowl, mix together the almond flour, polenta, baking soda, and salt.

2. In another small bowl, whisk together 3 tablespoons olive oil, lemon juice, lemon zest, egg, honey, and vanilla. Add the olive oil mixture to the flour mixture, and stir gently just until combined.

3. Line a 5-inch (12.5cm) round cake pan with a parchment paper round. (You can use a push-bottom pan for easier removal.) Grease the sides of the pan with the remaining ½ teaspoon olive oil, and pour in the batter.

4. Place the steam rack in the inner pot and add 1 cup water. Place the pan on the steam rack, uncovered. Lock the lid, and set the steam release valve to the sealing position. Select **Pressure Cook (High),** and set the cook time for **35 minutes.**

5. Once the cook time is complete, allow the pressure to release naturally for 5 minutes, then quick release any remaining pressure. Carefully remove the lid so as not to let condensation fall directly onto the cake.

6. Allow the cake to cool in the pan on a wire rack for 10 minutes. Remove the cake from the pan and invert onto the wire rack (the flat bottom of the cake now becomes the top), and allow to cool for 10 minutes more.

7. Transfer the cake to a serving plate and dust with powdered sugar. Cut into 6 wedges and serve immediately. Store any leftovers in an airtight container in the refrigerator for up to 3 days. Refresh each slice by placing in the microwave for a few seconds before serving.

TIP | For an orange polenta cake variation, replace the lemon juice and lemon zest with equal amounts of orange juice and orange zest.

NUTRITION PER SERVING:
Calories **166** • Total Fat **9.4g** • Total Carb **19g** • Fiber **0g** • Total Sugars **12g** • Protein **3g**

Simply Indulgent
Mini–Mason Jar Cupcakes

PROGRAM
Pressure Cook (High)

RELEASE
Natural and Quick

Gluten-Free

These grain-free cupcakes with rich chocolate ganache are an indulgence, pure and simple. While they shouldn't be everyday treats, these colorful cupcakes are perfectly suited for a mini celebration and are sure to make the occasion extra special!

Makes **4 cupcakes**   Serving Size **2 cupcakes**   Prep Time **10 mins**   Pressure Time **13 mins**   Total Time **1 hour 30 mins**

2 tsp salted butter, melted

¼ cup sour cream

½ tsp pure vanilla extract

1 large egg yolk

3 tbsp granulated sugar

⅓ cup (43g) cassava flour

1 tbsp (7g) blanched
almond flour

¼ tsp baking soda

Pinch of salt

1 tsp rainbow sprinkles
(optional), divided

For the ganache:
3 tbsp semisweet chocolate
chips

1 tbsp heavy whipping cream

1. Place the steam rack in the inner pot and add 1 cup water. Prepare the ganache. In a small stainless steel pan, combine the chocolate chips and heavy whipping cream. Place the pan on the steam rack. Lock the lid and set the steam release valve to the sealing position. Select **Pressure Cook (High),** and set the cook time for **1 minute.**

2. Once the cook time is complete, quick release the pressure. Press **Cancel** to turn off Keep Warm. Remove the pan from the inner pot and stir until smooth. Refrigerate for 30 minutes while preparing the cupcakes.

3. In a small bowl, whisk together the butter, sour cream, vanilla, egg yolk, and sugar. In a separate small bowl, stir together the cassava flour, almond flour, baking soda, and salt. Gently stir the flour mixture into the wet mixture, just until combined. Fold in ¾ teaspoon sprinkles, if using.

4. Spray 4 (4fl oz; 120ml) canning jars with nonstick spray, and gently divide the batter between them. Place the jars on the steam rack and rest the flat canning lid on top of each to keep out excess moisture. (There is no need to screw on the ring.) Lock the lid and set the steam release valve to the sealing position. Select **Pressure Cook (High),** and set the cook time for **12 minutes.**

5. Once the cook time is complete, quick release the pressure. Allow the cupcakes to cool, uncovered, in the jars on a wire rack for 10 minutes. Run a butter knife around the inside edges of the jars to make them easier to remove. Pop them out of the jars and place them on the wire racks until completely cooled, about 30 minutes.

6. Remove the chilled frosting and beat with a spoon for about 1 minute until it slightly lightens in color and becomes fluffy and spreadable. Spread or pipe onto the fully cooled cupcakes. Top with the remaining ¼ teaspoon sprinkles, if desired, and serve. Store leftovers in an airtight container in the refrigerator for up to 3 days.

NUTRITION PER SERVING:
Calories **392** • Total Fat **18.5g** • Total Carb **55g** • Fiber **4g** • Total Sugars **32g** • Protein **5g**

Talia's Fudge-A-Licious Brownies

PROGRAM
Pressure Cook (High)

RELEASE
Natural and Quick

Gluten-Free

One bite into these delectable (and surprisingly grain-free) brownies, and you'll surely swoon. Treat yourself to all the goodness of freshly baked brownies without a cake pan full of leftovers calling your name afterward. This recipe makes moderation easy!

Serves **4**   Serving Size **¼ pan**   Prep Time **10 mins**   Pressure Time **45 mins**   Total Time **1 hour 20 mins**

2oz (55g) semisweet chocolate chips

3 tbsp salted butter

⅓ cup granulated sugar

1 large egg

1 tsp pure vanilla extract

⅓ cup (43g) cassava flour

4 tsp Dutch-processed cocoa powder

¼ tsp baking soda

¼ tsp salt

1. In a small glass bowl, microwave the chocolate chips and butter on high for 30 seconds. Stir until smooth. Add the sugar, egg, and vanilla, and beat with a whisk until combined.

2. In a separate bowl, stir together the cassava flour, cocoa, baking soda, and salt. Add the flour mixture to the chocolate mixture, and stir until just combined.

3. Line a 5-inch (12.5cm) round cake pan with a parchment paper round. (You can use a push-bottom pan for easier removal.) Spray the sides of the pan with nonstick spray, and pour in the batter. Cover the top tightly with aluminum foil.

4. Place the steam rack in the inner pot and add 1 cup water. Place the pan on the steam rack. Lock the lid and set the steam release valve to the sealing position. Select **Pressure Cook (High),** and set the cook time for **45 minutes.**

5. Once the cook time is complete, allow the pressure to release naturally for 5 minutes, then quick release any remaining pressure. Allow the brownies to cool in the pan on a wire rack for at least 15 minutes. Cut into four wedges and serve warm or completely cooled. Store leftovers in an airtight container at room temperature for up to 3 days.

TIP For a nutty variation, add 2 tablespoons chopped walnuts or pecans to the batter.

For best results, use a food scale to accurately measure flours. If you do not have a food scale, gently spoon the flour into your measuring cup so as not to compact it. Inaccurately measuring flour can leave you with a hard and dense finished product.

NUTRITION PER SERVING:
Calories **273** • Total Fat **14.1g** • Total Carb **36g** • Fiber **3g** • Total Sugars **25g** • Protein **3g**

Blank Slate Cheesecake Cups

PROGRAM
Pressure Cook (Low)

RELEASE
Natural and Quick

Gluten-Free, Keto-Friendly Variation

Think of this recipe as an empty canvas ready for you to express all of your sweet inclinations. Try something classic like a drizzle of chocolate fudge or cherry pie filling, or go wild with off-the-wall flavors like huckleberry or maple bacon!

Makes **2 cheesecake cups** • Serving Size **1 cheesecake cup** • Prep Time **10 mins** • Pressure Time **12 mins** • Total Time **3 hours**

5oz (140g) cream cheese, room temperature

2 tbsp plain full-fat Greek yogurt

½ tsp pure vanilla extract

Pinch of salt

2 tbsp granulated sugar

1 large egg yolk

1. In a small bowl, stir the cream cheese with a spoon until soft and smooth. If it is too stiff to stir easily, allow it to sit at room temperature for a bit longer to soften.

2. Add the yogurt, vanilla, salt, and sugar, and mix until smooth. Add the egg yolk and gently mix just until combined, but do not overmix.

3. Spray 2 (8fl oz; 235ml) wide-mouth canning jars with nonstick spray, and pour half of the batter into each.

4. Place the steam rack in the inner pot and add 1 cup water. Place the jars on the steam rack and rest the flat canning lid on top of each to keep out excess moisture. (There is no need to screw on the ring.) Lock the lid and set the steam release valve to the sealing position. Select **Pressure Cook (Low),** and set the cook time for **12 minutes.**

5. Once the cook time is complete, allow the pressure to release naturally for 5 minutes, then quick release any remaining pressure. Remove the lids and allow the cheesecake cups to cool on a wire rack for 30 minutes. Cover, and refrigerate for at least 2 hours before serving.

TIP Make it keto friendly: Cutting sugar? Easily replace the sugar with the equivalent amount of your favorite sugar-free granulated sweetener.

There are two essential steps to achieving a perfectly creamy and lump-free cheesecake in the Instant Pot. The first is making sure that you bring the cream cheese to room temperature before starting. The second is to make sure that not don't overmix the batter after you've added the egg yolk.

NUTRITION PER SERVING:

Calories **344** • Total Fat **27.5g** • Total Carb **18g** • Fiber **0g** • Total Sugars **16g** • Protein **7g**

Matcha Mini Cheesecake

Matcha is purported to have numerous health benefits ranging from enhancing brain function to boosting detoxification. Adding this antioxidant powerhouse to your diet is easy and tasty with this decadently creamy, vibrant green dessert.

PROGRAM
Pressure Cook (Low)

RELEASE
Natural and Quick

Gluten-Free

Serves **4**   Serving Size **¼ cheesecake**   Prep Time **20 mins**   Pressure Time **30 mins**   Total Time **4 hours 30 mins**

¼ cup fresh raspberries (optional), for garnish

For the crust:
2 tsp salted butter, melted, plus more for greasing

⅓ cup crushed gluten-free gingersnap cookies (very fine crumbs)

For the filling:
8oz (225g) ⅓-less-fat cream cheese, room temperature

3 tbsp plain 0% milkfat Greek yogurt

¼ cup granulated sugar

1 tsp pure vanilla extract

⅛ tsp lemon zest

1 tbsp matcha green tea powder (culinary grade)

Pinch of salt

2 large egg yolks

1. Prepare the crust. In a small bowl, combine the butter and gingersnap cookie crumbs. Line a 4-inch (10cm) push-bottom cake pan with a parchment paper round, and grease the sides of the pan with butter. Evenly and firmly press the crust mixture into the bottom of the pan. Freeze for 10 minutes.

2. While the crust is chilling, prepare the filling. In a small bowl, stir the cream cheese with a spoon until soft and smooth. If it is too stiff to stir easily, allow it to sit at room temperature for a bit longer to soften.

3. Add the yogurt, sugar, vanilla, lemon zest, matcha, and salt. Mix until smooth. Add the egg yolks and gently mix just until combined, but do not overmix. Spread the cheesecake filling over the chilled crust and tap the pan on the counter several times to release any air bubbles. Cover the top tightly with foil.

4. Place the steam rack in the inner pot and add 1 cup water. Place the pan on the steam rack. Lock the lid and set the steam release valve to the sealing position. Select **Pressure Cook (Low),** and set the cook time for **30 minutes.**

5. Once the cook time is complete, allow the pressure to release naturally for 5 minutes, then quick release any remaining pressure. Allow the cheesecake to cool, uncovered, on a wire rack for 30 minutes. Cover and refrigerate for at least 3 hours. Cut into quarters, garnish with fresh raspberries, if desired, and serve.

TIP   If you can't find gluten-free gingersnaps, substitute with gluten-free graham crackers, adding ½ teaspoon ginger powder to the crumbs for that ginger kick.

Matcha not your cup of tea? Make this into a coffee cheesecake. Substitute instant espresso powder for the matcha. Omit the lemon zest. Use gluten-free graham cracker or chocolate cookie crumbs for the crust. Garnish with dark chocolate shavings.

To make the pan easier to remove from the Instant Pot after cooking, make a sling for your pan with foil (page 13).

NUTRITION PER SERVING (EXCLUDING RASPBERRIES):
Calories **305** • Total Fat **15.4g** • Total Carb **33g** • Fiber **1g** • Total Sugars **20g** • Protein **8g**

Pineapple Upside-Down Mason Jar Cakes

PROGRAM
Pressure Cook (High)

RELEASE
Natural and Quick

Gluten-Free

Pineapple rings are perfectly sized to fit down in the bottom of a mason jar and make these adorable, personal-sized upside-down cakes. The coconut sugar and butter combine to coat everything with a sticky sweet topping that brings this dessert together.

Makes **2 cakes**   Serving Size **1 cake**   Prep Time **10 mins**   Pressure Time **18 mins**   Total Time **1 hour**

2 tbsp salted butter, melted

¼ cup coconut sugar

2 canned pineapple rings

2 maraschino cherries (optional)

¼ cup plain full-fat Greek yogurt

1 tsp pure vanilla extract

1 large egg yolk

1 tbsp pineapple juice (from the can of pineapple rings)

⅓ cup (43g) cassava flour

1 tbsp (7g) blanched almond flour

¼ tsp baking soda

Pinch of salt

1. In a medium bowl, whisk together the butter and coconut sugar. Spread 2 teaspoons of the butter-sugar mixture into each of 2 (8fl oz; 235ml) wide-mouth canning jars.

2. Place a pineapple ring into each jar on top of the butter and sugar mixture, and place 1 cherry (if using) in the center of each ring. Set the jars aside.

3. To the bowl of the remaining butter-sugar mixture, add the Greek yogurt, vanilla, egg yolk, and pineapple juice, and whisk until smooth.

4. In another small bowl, stir together the cassava flour, almond flour, baking soda, and salt. Add the flour mixture to the yogurt mixture, and stir until just combined. Divide the batter between the jars and spread out gently.

5. Place the steam rack in the inner pot and add 1 cup water. Place the jars on the steam rack and rest the flat canning lid on top of each to keep out excess moisture. (There is no need to screw on the ring.)

6. Lock the lid and set the steam release valve to the sealing position. Select **Pressure Cook (High),** and set the cook time for **18 minutes.**

7. Once the cook time is complete, allow the pressure to release naturally for 5 minutes, then quickly release any remaining pressure.

8. Allow the cakes to cool in the jars on a wire rack for 5 minutes. Run a butter knife around the inside edges of the jars to make them easier to remove, and turn them out onto a serving tray. The pineapple ring will now be the top of the cake. Allow to cool for 5 more minutes before serving.

TIP | For best results, use a food scale to accurately measure flours. If you do not have a food scale, gently spoon the flour into your measuring cup so as not to compact it. Inaccurately measuring flour can leave you with a hard and dense finished product.

NUTRITION PER SERVING:
Calories **302** • Total Fat **12.1g** • Total Carb **48g** • Fiber **3g** • Total Sugars **27g** • Protein **3g**

Nutty Mason Jar Carrot Cakes

These little cakes are deliciously spiced and chock-full of healthy walnuts and shredded carrots. A generous smear of cream cheese frosting adds the finishing touch. Pair with a cup of coffee for a perfect after-dinner indulgence.

PROGRAM
Pressure Cook (High)

RELEASE
Natural and Quick

Gluten-Free, Dairy-Free Variation

Makes **2 cakes**   Serving Size **1 cake**   Prep Time **15 mins**   Pressure Time **18 mins**   Total Time **1 hour 10 mins**

1 tbsp melted coconut oil, slightly cooled

¼ cup unsweetened applesauce

1 tsp pure vanilla extract

1 large egg white

3 tbsp coconut sugar

2 tbsp finely chopped walnuts

¼ cup shredded carrot

⅓ cup (43g) cassava flour

2 tbsp (14g) blanched almond flour

¼ tsp baking soda

Pinch of salt

½ tsp ground cinnamon

⅛ tsp ground ginger

⅛ tsp ground allspice

⅛ tsp cardamom powder

For the frosting:
2 tbsp cream cheese

2 tsp powdered sugar

1 tsp half & half

1. In a medium bowl, whisk together the coconut oil, applesauce, vanilla, egg white, and coconut sugar. Stir in the walnuts and shredded carrots.

2. In another small bowl, stir together the cassava flour, almond flour, baking soda, salt, cinnamon, ginger, allspice, and cardamom. Add the flour mixture to the carrot mixture and stir until just combined.

3. Spray 2 (8fl oz; 235ml) wide-mouth canning jars with nonstick spray, and gently spread half of the batter into each. Place the steam rack in the inner pot and add 1 cup water. Place the jars on the steam rack and rest the flat canning lid on top of each to keep out excess moisture. (There is no need to screw on the ring.) Lock the lid and set the steam release valve to the sealing position. Select **Pressure Cook (High),** and set the cook time for **18 minutes.**

4. While the cakes are cooking, prepare the frosting. In a small microwave-safe bowl, add the cream cheese. Microwave in 5-second intervals, stirring after each one, until the cream cheese has softened and is very easy to stir with a spoon. Add the powdered sugar and the half & half, and stir together until smooth. Set aside.

5. Once the cook time is complete, allow the pressure to release naturally for 5 minutes, then quick release any remaining pressure. Allow the cakes to cool in the jars on a wire rack for 20 minutes. When cool, spread half of the frosting onto each cake and serve immediately in the jars.

TIP | Make it dairy-free: Substitute your favorite vegan cream cheese for the regular cream cheese.

For best results, use a food scale to accurately measure flours. If you do not have a food scale, gently spoon the flour into your measuring cup so as not to compact it. Inaccurately measuring flour can leave you with a hard and dense finished product.

NUTRITION PER SERVING:
Calories **341** • Total Fat **17.5g** • Total Carb **44g** • Fiber **4g** • Total Sugars **21g** • Protein **7g**

Mochaccino Lava Cake

PROGRAM
Pressure Cook (High)

RELEASE
Quick

Gluten-Free

Easily whip up this gooey, decadent treat at a moment's notice. It is sure to prove once and for all that there is no need to settle for suboptimal desserts while eating a gluten-free diet.

Makes **2 lava cakes**   Serving Size **1 lava cake**   Prep Time **10 mins**   Pressure Time **8 mins**   Total Time **28 mins**

2 tbsp semisweet chocolate chips

5 tbsp white chocolate chips, divided

2 tbsp butter

3 tbsp (24g) cassava flour

1 large egg, lightly beaten

2 tsp heavy whipping cream

¾ tsp instant espresso powder

Powdered sugar (optional), for serving

1. In a small glass bowl, microwave the semisweet chocolate chips, 3 tablespoons white chocolate chips, and butter on high for 15-second intervals, stirring between intervals, until melted and smooth.

2. Add the cassava flour and egg, and mix until combined. Spray 2 (4fl oz; 120ml) canning jars with nonstick spray. Pour half of the chocolate batter into each.

3. In a separate small glass bowl, stir together the remaining 2 tablespoons white chocolate chips, heavy whipping cream, and instant espresso powder. Microwave on high for 15-second intervals, stirring between intrevals, until smooth.

4. Add half of the white chocolate–espresso mixture to each jar, carefully dropping each spoonful directly onto the center of the chocolate batter— this will form the "lava" core. There is no need to cover the "lava" with cake batter as the batter will rise and cover it as the cake cooks.

5. Place the steam rack in the inner pot and add 1 cup water. Place the jars, uncovered, on the steam rack. Lock the lid and set the steam release valve to the sealing position. Select **Pressure Cook (High),** and set the cook time for **8 minutes.**

6. Once the cook time is complete, quick release the pressure. Allow the lava cakes to cool on a wire rack for 5 minutes. Run a butter knife around the inside edges of the jars to make them easier to remove, if desired, and turn them out onto a serving tray. Dust with powdered sugar, if desired, and serve immediately.

TIP | For a classic chocolate lava cake, use semisweet chocolate chips in place of the white chocolate chips and reduce the instant espresso powder to ¼ teaspoon.

NUTRITION PER SERVING:

Calories **389** • Total Fat **27.3g** • Total Carb **32g** • Fiber **1g** • Total Sugars **31g** • Protein **1g**

Index

A

aluminum foil, 13
anti-block shield, 9
appetizers and snacks
  Bacon and Bleu Cheese–
    Stuffed Mushroom Caps,
    132–133
  Basil and Greek Olive White
    Bean Dip, 135
  Brown Rice Dolmas, 122
  Cheesy Taco Dip, 134
  Creamy Pesto Chicken Dip,
    136–137
  Meat Lovers Crustless Mini
    Quiche Bites, 123
  Mexican Stuffed Mini
    Peppers, 128–129
  Mini–Mason Jar Corn Dog
    Muffins, 130
  Mu Shu Vegetable
    Dumplings, 127
  Pickled Jalapeño Deviled
    Eggs, 120–121
  Renae's Favorite Hummus,
    131
  Steamed Pork and Ginger
    Dumplings, 126
  Sweet and Sour Danish
    Cabbage, 124–125
Artichokes with Garlic-Herb
  Butter, 112
Asian Chicken Lettuce Wraps,
  48–49
Asian Plum Short Ribs, 51
Autumn Pumpkin Chili, 78–79

B

Bacon and Bleu Cheese–
  Stuffed Mushroom Caps,
  132–133
Bacon and Mushroom–
  Covered Pork Chops, 55
baked goods, 14
Banana Chocolate Chip Mason
  Jar Muffins, 30
base (cooker), 9
Basil and Greek Olive White
  Bean Dip, 135
Bean/Grain/Chili program, 11
Beef Stew with Parsnips, 74
Blank Slate Cheesecake
  Cups, 151

Blueberry Greek Yogurt Mason
  Jar Coffee Cakes, 31
breakfast
  Banana Chocolate Chip
    Mason Jar Muffins, 30
  Blueberry Greek Yogurt
    Mason Jar Coffee Cakes,
    31
  For-Charity Buttermilk
    Pancake Bites, 34
  Coconut Currant Breakfast
    Quinoa, 24
  Down-Home Cheesy Grits
    with a Kick, 22–23
  Easy-Peel Hard-Boiled
    Eggs, 39
  Honey Lemon Mini–Mason
    Jar Muffins, 28–29
  Honeyed Apple Oatmeal, 20
  Levi's Chia Applesauce Baby
    Bundtlet, 32–33
  Maple Buckwheat Hot
    Cereal with Hemp
    Hearts, 21
  Orange Marmalade, 26
  Poached Salmon and Eggs
    with Yogurt Sauce, 35
  From-Scratch Vanilla Bean
    Yogurt, 25
  Spiced Chai, 27
  Spinach Prosciutto Egg
    Bites, 38
  Sticky Plantain and Bacon
    Steel-Cut Oatmeal, 18–19
  Sweet Potato Breakfast Egg
    Cups, 36–37
Brown Rice Dolmas, 122
Buffalo Chicken–Stuffed Sweet
  Potatoes, 56–57
Bundt pans (3-cup), 13

C

canning jars (8fl oz), 13
canning jelly jars (4fl oz), 13
Caribbean-Inspired Pork and
  Plantain Stew, 82–83
Cheesy Broccoli and Rice
  Soup, 87
Cheesy Taco Dip, 134
Chicken Bone Broth, 44
Chocolate Fondue Dip, 143

Christmas Eve Cinnamon Rice
  Pudding, 146
Cinnamon Apple Pork
  Tenderloin, 54
Classic Beef Stroganoff, 75
Coconut Currant Breakfast
  Quinoa, 24
condensation collector, 9
cook times, 15
cooker base, 9
Cornbread Bundtlet, 117
Cranberry Apple Quinoa
  Pilaf, 101
Cranberry Chicken, 52–53
Creamy Corn Chowder, 76
Creamy Pesto Chicken Dip,
  136–137
Curried Cauliflower with
  Raisins and Almonds, 100
Cut-the-Carbs Spaghetti
  Squash, 104

D

desserts
  Blank Slate Cheesecake
    Cups, 151
  Chocolate Fondue Dip, 143
  Christmas Eve Cinnamon
    Rice Pudding, 146
  Drunken Apples with
    Whiskey and Raisins,
    140–141
  Honey-Vanilla Peach
    Topping, 142
  Lemon Olive Oil Polenta
    Cake, 147
  Matcha Mini Cheesecake,
    152–153
  Mochaccino Lava Cake,
    156–157
  Nutty Mason Jar Carrot
    Cakes, 155
  Pineapple Upside-Down
    Mason Jar Cakes, 154
  Simply Indulgent Mini–
    Mason Jar Cupcakes,
    148–149
  Sticky Coconut Rice with
    Mango, 144–145
  Talia's Fudge-a-Licious
    Brownies, 150
doubling recipes, 15

Down-Home Cheesy Grits with
  a Kick, 22–23
Drunken Apples with Whiskey
  and Raisins, 140–141

E

Easy Potato Cauliflower
  Mash, 108
Easy-Peel Hard-Boiled
  Eggs, 39
egg bite molds, 12
Egg Drop Soup, 85
Egg program, 11
egg steamer trivets with tall
  legs, 12
entrées
  Asian Chicken Lettuce
    Wraps, 48–49
  Asian Plum Short Ribs, 51
  Bacon and Mushroom–
    Covered Pork Chops, 55
  Buffalo Chicken–Stuffed
    Sweet Potatoes, 56–57
  Cinnamon Apple Pork
    Tenderloin, 54
  Classic Beef Stroganoff, 75
  Cranberry Chicken, 52–53
  Garlic Butter Shrimp
    Scampi, 62–63
  German Sausage and
    Sauerkraut Dinner, 58
  Greek Chicken Gyro Bowls,
    42–43
  Layered Chicken Enchilada
    Casserole, 45
  Lime-Cilantro Pulled
    Pork, 50
  Massaman Chicken Curry,
    72–73
  One-Pot Chicken Teriyaki
    and Rice, 65
  One-Pot Pad Thai, 70
  One-Pot Red Beans and
    Rice, 64
  Orange Marmalade Chicken,
    60
  Restaurant-Style Ramen
    Bowls, 68–69
  Rotisserie-Style Chicken and
    Lemony Rice, 46
  Taco Meatloaf Cups, 47
  Tangy Beef and Broccoli, 59
  Thai Peanut Pork Curry, 71

Zuppa Toscana One-Pot Pasta, 61
equipment, 12–13

F

float valve, 9
Fluffy Brown Rice, 95
For-Charity Buttermilk Pancake Bites, 34
From-Scratch Vanilla Bean Yogurt, 25

G

Garlic Butter Shrimp Scampi, 62–63
German Sausage and Sauerkraut Dinner, 58
grains, 14
Greek Chicken Gyro Bowls, 42–43
Green Chile Pork and Potato Stew, 86

H–I

Harvest Apple Butternut Squash Soup, 90
Honey Lemon Mini–Mason Jar Muffins, 28–29
Honeyed Apple Oatmeal, 20
Honey-Vanilla Peach Topping, 142
Hungarian Mushroom Soup, 91

inner pot, 9

J–K–L

Jalapeño Popper Soup with Sausage, 88–89

Keep Warm program, 11
Kimchi Fried Rice, 98–99

Layered Chicken Enchilada Casserole, 45
Lemon Dill Creamer Potatoes, 106–107
Lemon Olive Oil Polenta Cake, 147
Lemony Cauliflower Tabbouleh, 102–103
Levi's Chia Applesauce Baby Bundtlet, 32–33
lid, 9
Lime-Cilantro Pulled Pork, 50

M

Maple Buckwheat Hot Cereal with Hemp Hearts, 21
Maple-Glazed Brussels Sprouts, 113
Massaman Chicken Curry, 72–73
Matcha Mini Cheesecake, 152–153
Meat Lovers Crustless Mini Quiche Bites, 123
meats, 14
Meat/Stew program, 11
Mexican Stuffed Mini Peppers, 128–129
Mini Instant Pot
    anti-block shield, 9
    baked goods, 14
    choosing model, 8
    condensation collector, 9
    cooker base, 9
    doubling recipes, 15
    float valve, 9
    grains, 14
    inner pot, 9
    lid, 9
    meats, 14
    nutritional benefits, 8
    programs, 11
    quick release button, 9
    sealing ring, 9
    servings, 8
    steam release valve, 9
    timing, 15
    troubleshooting, 15
    vegetables, 15
Mini–Mason Jar Corn Dog Muffins, 130
Minnesota Wild Rice Soup with Bacon, 67
Mochaccino Lava Cake, 156–157
models, Mini Instant Pot, 8
Mu Shu Vegetable Dumplings, 127

N

No-Dairy New England Clam Chowder, 77
No-Fuss Black Beans, 109
nonpressure programs, 11
Nourishing Chicken Noodle Soup, 84
nutritional benefits, 8
Nutty Mason Jar Carrot Cakes, 155

O

One-Pot Chicken Teriyaki and Rice, 65
One-Pot Pad Thai, 70
One-Pot Red Beans and Rice, 64
Orange Marmalade, 26
Orange Marmalade Chicken, 60
oven-safe bowls (1-quart), 12

P

pan slings, 13
pans, 12
Parmesan Green Beans with Bacon, 114–115
Pickled Jalapeño Deviled Eggs, 120–121
Pineapple Upside-Down Mason Jar Cakes, 154
plum sauce, 51
poached eggs, 35
Poached Salmon and Eggs with Yogurt Sauce, 35
Porridge/Oatmeal program, 11
potholders, 13
pot-in-pot cooking method, 21
Pot-in-Pot White Rice, 94
pressure, cooking under, 8, 10
Pressure Cook program, 11
pressure programs, 11
prewashed quinoa, 24
programs, 11

Q

Quick Cauliflower Rice, 96
quick release button, 9
quinoa, prewashed, 24
Quinoa in a Snap, 97

R

Red Lentil Chicken Stew with Quinoa, 81
Renae's Favorite Hummus, 131
Restaurant-Style Ramen Bowls, 68–69
Rice program, 11
Rotisserie-Style Chicken and Lemony Rice, 46

S

Sauté program, 11
sealing, versus venting, 9

sealing ring, 9
sides
    Artichokes with Garlic-Herb Butter, 112
    Cornbread Bundtlet, 117
    Cranberry Apple Quinoa Pilaf, 101
    Curried Cauliflower with Raisins and Almonds, 100
    Cut-the-Carbs Spaghetti Squash, 104
    Easy Potato Cauliflower Mash, 108
    Fluffy Brown Rice, 95
    Kimchi Fried Rice, 98–99
    Lemon Dill Creamer Potatoes, 106–107
    Lemony Cauliflower Tabbouleh, 102–103
    Maple-Glazed Brussels Sprouts, 113
    No-Fuss Black Beans, 109
    Parmesan Green Beans with Bacon, 114–115
    Pot-in-Pot White Rice, 94
    Quick Cauliflower Rice, 96
    Quinoa in a Snap, 97
    Soy Ginger–Glazed Carrots, 110–111
    Sweet and Sour Danish Cabbage, 116
    Tuscan Polenta, 105
silicone egg bite molds, 12
Simply Indulgent Mini–Mason Jar Cupcakes, 148–149
slow cook program, 11
smoked gouda, 38
snacks. *see* appetizers and snacks
soups and stews
    Autumn Pumpkin Chili, 78–79
    Beef Stew with Parsnips, 74
    Caribbean-Inspired Pork and Plantain Stew, 82–83
    Cheesy Broccoli and Rice Soup, 87
    Chicken Bone Broth, 44
    Creamy Corn Chowder, 76
    Egg Drop Soup, 85
    Green Chile Pork and Potato Stew, 86
    Harvest Apple Butternut Squash Soup, 90
    Hungarian Mushroom Soup, 91

Jalapeño Popper Soup with Sausage, 88–89

Minnesota Wild Rice Soup with Bacon, 67

No-Dairy New England Clam Chowder, 77

Nourishing Chicken Noodle Soup, 84

Red Lentil Chicken Stew with Quinoa, 81

Vegetarian Curried Lentil Stew, 66

White Chicken Chili, 80

Soup/Broth program, 11

Soy Ginger–Glazed Carrots, 110–111

Spiced Chai, 27

Spinach Prosciutto Egg Bites, 38

stackable pans, 12

Steam program, 11

steam racks, 13

steam release valve, 9

Steamed Pork and Ginger Dumplings, 126

steamer baskets with feet, 12

Sticky Coconut Rice with Mango, 144–145

Sticky Plantain and Bacon Steel-Cut Oatmeal, 18–19

Sweet and Sour Danish Cabbage, 116

Sweet Chili Chicken Meatballs, 124–125

Sweet Potato Breakfast Egg Cups, 36–37

sweet potatoes, cook time, 56

T

Taco Meatloaf Cups, 47

Talia's Fudge-a-Licious Brownies, 150

Tangy Beef and Broccoli, 59

Thai Peanut Pork Curry, 71

timing, 15

troubleshooting, 15

Tuscan Polenta, 105

V

vegetables, 15

Vegetarian Curried Lentil Stew, 66

venting, versus sealing, 9

W–X–Y–Z

White Chicken Chili, 80

wide-mouth canning jars (8fl oz), 13

wild rice, freezing, 67

Yogurt program, 11

Zuppa Toscana One-Pot Pasta, 61

Acknowledgments

First and foremost I would like to thank my daughter, Autumn Barrett, for washing the never-ending pile of dishes that came along with the writing of this cookbook. I would not have wanted to attempt this without you.

Thank you to my amazing husband, Jeff Barrett, who supported me and encouraged me to take on this project from the beginning, even when I was unsure of my ability. Also to my children, Autumn, Talia, Charity, Renae, and Levi Barrett, who cheered me on and gave me endless inspiration during the long months of recipe development, as well as all of their professional taste-testing opinions. You had to endure many nights of very odd dinner combinations as these recipes were coming together, and all of your thumbs-up and thumbs-down helped shape this book into what it is.

To all of my subscribers on YouTube, without you, this cookbook would never have become a reality. Your enthusiasm, questions, feedback, and encouragement are what continue spur me on to crafting new recipes to share and plumbing the depths of what an Instant Pot can do.

Finally, to the team at Alpha Books, and especially to Alexandra Andrzejewski, thank you for giving me this incredible opportunity and for your tireless support and guidance from start to finish. You made a complex and overwhelming process not only manageable but an absolute joy. It has been an honor to work with such a talented and professional group of people on this project.

About the Author

Nili Barrett has been sharing her love for cooking healthy and creative meals via her YouTube channel—Indigo Nili—since 2011, and she runs the recipe blog IndigoNili.com. Nili's adventures as a stay-at-home mother of five have received millions of views online, and her talent for creating both original and classic dishes for specific dietary needs has made her an important guide for many looking to escape the standard American diet.